W9-BZF-869

Modern Prints

Printmaking, in which an artist conceives an image with the intention of multiplying it, has been called 'the democratic art', and certainly the editioning of an artist's work by any of the print processes makes it accessible to a wider public by virtue not only of increased quantity, but of decreased cost. The decline of conventional patronage, the expansion of the art market, the gradual rise of a better educated and better paid general public, enthusiastic to understand and perhaps collect art, together with the artist's fascination for exploring media and interchanging art forms, has given a special relevance to prints in the twentieth century.

This book traces the history of printmaking from the demise of hand-done reproductive engraving at the end of the nineteenth century to the explosion in size, colour and technical invention characterizing the boom in artists' prints following World War II. The author discusses the concept of the 'original print' (the etching, lithograph or woodcut conceived and hand worked by the artist himself but often editioned in a limited number by craftsmen) and pays particular attention to the way prints have evolved in the 1960s (influenced by a machine technology), to a state in which photographic, non-gestural or processed images are creatively combined in prints specified by the artist, but often entirely realized by master printers, and susceptible to mass production.

Pat Gilmour, a lecturer in printmaking and art history in a London Further Education College, contributes a regular column on graphics to *Arts Review*, and also writes for *Art and Artists*.

Front cover
Matisse *Head c.* 1948
Sugar aquatint, edition 25, courtesy Lumley Cazalet Ltd, London

Marjan Pogačnik *Unseen by the Roadside* 1967
Intaglio, courtesy Ljubljana Biennale

Modern Prints

Pat Gilmour

General Editor David Herbert

Studio Vista | Dutton Pictureback

To Alex

Acknowledgments The author is indebted to innumerable galleries, publishers and artists who provided information and photographs of the works illustrated; to Stanley Jones of Curwen, Christopher Prater of Kelpra, and Ken Tyler of Gemini for technical information; to Robert Erskine who generously gave access to material concerning the St George's Gallery; to the organizers of Xylon and Ljubljana, Tokyo, Venice and Bradford Biennales; to Pam and Henri Edion, C. E. Waller, and John Gainsborough of *Arts Review,* who kindly read proofs; and last but not least, Allan Perry who gave continual help, including two fingers on a second typewriter at the eleventh hour.

© Pat Gilmour 1970
Designed by Gillian Greenwood
Published in Great Britain by Studio Vista Limited,
Blue Star House, Highgate Hill, London N19
and in the USA by E. P. Dutton and Co. Inc.
201 Park Avenue South, New York 3, New York
Set in Univers 8 on 11 pt
Made and printed in Great Britain by
Richard Clay (The Chaucer Press) Limited
Bungay, Suffolk

SBN 289 79716 0 (paperback)
    289 79717 9 (hardback)

Contents

INTRODUCTION

Of all English words, perhaps print is the most unsatisfactory. Its imprecision proves language a very blunt instrument.

Wearing a print dress, I print this manuscript that a typist may convert it to another form of print. The prints which are the subject of this book are artists' prints, by my definition images invented by an artist for multiplication; these must never be confused with wholly mechanical prints of oils or watercolours which the artist did not conceive for print, better called 'reproductions'. My description of autographic prints will appear in typographic print, illustrated by photographic prints, which have been reproduced by commercial line and half-tone block prints. The print thickens. . . .

Traditionally, artists' prints have been made by one of three basic processes: the *relief*, usually incised wood in which the image to be inked is left as an upstanding surface; the *intaglio*—etching and engraving—in which the design of tool-cut or acid-etched furrows recessed in a metal plate can be filled with a stiff ink and printed under great pressure once the surface of the plate has been wiped; and *surface* or *planographic* printing, in which a greasy image, worked on a stone slab or special plate, accepts ink, while the rest of the surface is treated to reject it, creating when impressed on paper, a lithograph.

All three methods existed as hand-done processes before commercial mass-production equivalents employing photo-processes were developed. Letterpress is essentially the equivalent of relief, rotogravure of intaglio, and offset lithography of surface printing. The fourth main process now used—screenprinting—is perhaps the most fascinating development. Stencilling, its simplest form, was known before any other printing process. It developed this century as a form of commercial printing and was then explored by artists, who saw it as the embodiment of the technological age.

If one looks at the history of hand-printed duplicable images, their use has been quantitatively more utilitarian than aesthetic. They have disseminated factual knowledge, and propagated religious belief and social and political criticism. Another of their huge functions has been to copy other works of art.

Although aesthetic quality has often been a concomitant of these utilitarian roles, the first fifty years of the twentieth century resulted in printmaking, freed by photomechanical process from the necessity of copying, establishing itself as a medium of aesthetic expression used for its own sake in a way previously rare.

Because its technical mastery frequently requires a very long apprenticeship, printmaking has often been divided into specialist tasks for three different people. The artist, print potential in mind, conceives the idea and possibly gives it shape in another medium; the tool-producer translates it into printable form on wood-block, metal, or stone; the artisan editions it.

This century, we have tended to idealize and set apart those artists, working alone and by hand, who have combined the first two and sometimes all three functions, maintaining that only their prints are in a special sense 'original'. Several committees between 1960 and 1965 tried variously to define, protect, and elevate the 'original' print, always equating it with artist handwork. But as the 1960s progressed, it became apparent that artists were eroding boundaries not only between traditional artforms, colouring sculptures and building paintings out into three dimensions, but also between all mark making conventions, and while the technically 'original' print could be little more than an artist's transposed drawing, or simulated painting, the photomechanical or commercial devices, outlawed by the committees, had great creative potential not exclusively depending on the artist grappling with all his materials himself.

Utamaro
(Left) *Youth and Girl*
(Right) *Courtesan with Tobacco Pipe c.* 1800
Woodcuts, unlimited editions, courtesy Anthony d'Offay, London

8

HISTORY

Nineteenth-century background to originality

The apogee of tripartite printmaking was the Japanese Ukiyo-e (Transient World) print, ephemeral, expendable, cheap, in which the idols of the day, from pretty girls to boxers, were recorded for the popular taste in a way then thought rather vulgar. In the west today, the surviving examples are rare, treasured, and expensive.

Perfectly understanding his medium, the artist would make a drawing which was pasted to the cherry wood to be cut by another, and printed by a third. Miracles of precision, with exquisite frond-cutting in the helicopter hair-dos. Utamaro pin-ups combined the refinements of uninked embossing, brass-dust sprinkled mica backgrounds, and lacquered areas glossing the rice paste inks.

'Who but the absurdest purist could frown at Utamaro or Hokusai,' asked Bliss in his *History of Wood Engraving*, 'because they did not do their own cutting?'

To mid-nineteenth-century France, where such prints arrived as wrapping round Eastern curios, their use of texture, pattern, and asymmetrical composition, their absence of mathematica perspective but suggestion of depth through aerial colour, mirror imagery, and transparency, proved liberating in the break with Renaissance tradition.

French etching and lithography had faltered frequently during the nineteenth century and although the greatest artists experimented in print techniques backed by publishers like Cadart, critics and collectors alike preferred works by rather feeble engravers interpreting paintings.

Francis Holl *Railway Station* after William Frith, RA, 1862
Engraving, courtesy Victoria and Albert Museum, London
Crown copyright reserved

In England, the position was the same. A whole school of reproductive steel engravers, copying oils by Royal Academicians now forgotten, satisfied the pictorial demands of the new Victorian middle class. Publishers paid enormous sums for engraving rights—Frith's *Railway Station*, £4,500 in 1860, earned Holl the engraver £2,000 for two years' work, and sold for £15 15s a signed proof.

That reproductive steel engravers were Royal Academy exhibitors while original etchers were rejected, was a thorn in the flesh of Seymour Haden, an English surgeon, who, with his brother-in-law Whistler, established a reverence for spontaneous

Seymour Haden *Egham Lock* 1864
Etching, courtesy William Weston Gallery, London

drawing on the plate. He was king-pin of the 1881 Society of Painter-Etchers, and gave a famous address in 1883 on 'The Relative Claims of Etching and Engraving to Rank as Fine Arts' (in which, it appeared, engraving had no claims) when he fumed and fulminated about the Royal Academy, and the lifeless formulae reproductive engravers applied, come flesh or foreground.

In his own skilful work progressively etching the accents in plates like *Egham Lock,* Haden emulated Rembrandt, a fore runner of the modern attitude, for whom he had a scholarly passion. Although some say Haden opposed limitation, a marketing device making a print rarer and therefore costlier to collectors,

Whistler left Paris for London with the idea of carefully printed limited editions and the two of them began signing proofs in pencil rather than in the plate. Indeed, Whistler would sell signed lithographs for £4 4s and unsigned ones for £2 2s, his autograph as valuable as his art. Both stressed the importance of the printing, and Haden recommended if etchers could not print their own plates, they should find a printer 'with the palm of a duchess'. By the end of the first quarter of the twentieth century etching was phenomenally popular, and the signed limited edition the norm; today, the difference between a signed and unsigned Chagall print can be several hundred pounds.

For some time before reproductive printers were replaced by the photo-engraved line and then the half-tone with its dot screen, the work of wood engravers for books and newspapers like the *Illustrated London News*, had declined. The handcraft had become as 'mechanical' whether servile cutters unintelligently reproduced the drawings of artists like Doré (who once indicated a repetition of windows by writing 'etc' and had the word cut in the block, to print back to front) or transferred to the block and imitated photographic tones. It was against such work that Gauguin reacted when he wrote to his friend de Monfried that wood engraving was losing its special characteristics and becoming every day 'more like photogravure . . . detestable'.

His own primitive woodcuts, inspired by Tahiti, lovely in their balancing of black and white, contrasted vigorous gouge-marks with delicately rendered greys from glasspapered and lowered surfaces, and he revitalized the medium, although few would pay the pittance he asked at the time.

Gauguin *Nave Nave Fenua* (*Terre delicieuse*) 1894/5, Woodcut, edition 100, courtesy Courtauld Institute, London

In 1889 the formation of the Peintres Graveurs Français reawoke interest, and publications such as *L'Estampe Originale* appeared. Toulouse Lautrec's lithograph, showing Jane Avril and Ancourt's master printer Père Cotelle at a lithographic press, was designed as a cover. Some contributers, regarding print as a device for reproducing drawings, handed another printer named Clot roughs both to draw on the stone and print as if their own work; contemporary definitions of 'originality' seek to prevent such malpractices. But Lautrec, his colour lithographs reflecting Japanese style in their fluent line, ingeniously created a tooth-brush-spattered drizzle of tone and exploited effects in the medium unobtainable in any other way.

Toulouse Lautrec *L'Estampe Originale* 1893
Lithograph, edition 100, courtesy London Arts

Edvard Munch *The Kiss* (4th version) 1902
Woodcut, courtesy Victorian and Albert Museum, London
Crown copyright reserved

Influenced by the Parisian *fin-de-siècle milieu*, the Norwegian Edvard Munch inspired, in his turn, the German Expressionists. Many of his graphic themes—his disturbing view of sex relationships, his anxious loneliness—repeat paintings, yet achieve greater force and clarity in print. The concept and the means fuse, and in a work like *The Kiss* (the innovatory overprinted plank grain of which still excites emulation) one perceives that the lovers, gouged from a single block, may be one flesh, but have also lost their identity. The print is a masterpiece in its own right, and has outgrown the portfolio.

Joseph Hecht *Paysage de Provence* 1925
Engraving, edition 30, courtesy Brook Street Gallery, London

The twentieth century

The graphic work of the German *Brücke* artists, stemming from
the pathfinding of Munch and Gauguin, reinforced the growing
concept of originality. Kirchner, whose 1,500 prints are sometimes
thought more significant than his painting, insisted that a work
was only original if the artist printed it himself. Certainly the
Brücke contributions to the politically disrupted and incompleted
Bauhaus portfolios of the 1920s were the most vivid, although
Feininger, in charge of the Bauhaus print workshop, ran them
close.

   In England the boom in mediocre topographical etching, un-
wittingly opened up by Whistler and Haden, at least had one good
result in enabling the young Anthony Gross to make a living sup-
plying a Strand printseller. In Paris, he met the Pole Joseph Hecht,
reinstating the engraving burin as a creative tool after Haden's

Anthony Gross *Pujols* 1932
Etching, edition 50

devastations, with delightful crystalline cuts transmitting the life force in growing things; and Hayter, destined to become the most technically inventive and influential painter-engraver of the twentieth century, learning the use of the burin from Hecht. Gross, however, deciding linear etching was his métier, abolished Rembrandtian cross-hatching from his work, and developed his distinctive lyrical approach to nature. A few relatives on the grass in *Pujols,* show a sensitivity to the poetry of the commonplace, and explain how he survived the financial crash of the 1930s, when the bottom dropped out of the etching market. Innovatory tooling wins a textural range from the delicacy of suede-soft grass to richly clotted leaves, and black ink on white paper (the height, some would say, of graphic art), provides him all the colour in the world.

17

Graham Sutherland *Meadow Chapel* 1928
Etching, courtesy Folio Fine Art, London

Graham Sutherland *Beetles I*
Indian ink and wash, 1965; and Lithograph, 1967, edition 70 from *The Bestiary*, courtesy Marlborough Fine Art Ltd, London

Graham Sutherland, who like Gross had a reputation for intaglio, is perhaps glad he did not survive the Depression, at any rate as an etcher. It deflected him from Palmer-inspired pastorals such as *Meadow Chapel*, to the painting which has since won him an international reputation.

Wassily Kandinsky noted in *Point, Line and Plane* in the 1920s that colour lithography was getting closer to painting, and Sutherland's experience in lithographic poster design before World War II stood him in good stead for the print renaissance which followed it. The preparatory wash drawing, reversed in the lithographic version of *Beetles I*, part of *The Bestiary*, a major portfolio of twenty-five prints, shows how amenable the painter may find lithography. But although one version may appear very like the other, reproduced in black and white, close attention to

the originals reveals how Sutherland transposes his preparatory gouaches into the special qualities of the print medium; the fine sensuous bloom of the lithographic wash played off against the granularity of broadside chalk, the transparent colours overprinting each other, and black, in subtle modification, with rubbings Max Ernst termed *frottages* transferred from special papers on to the zinc plates to provide textures.

It took Sutherland a whole year just to complete this work. Had he followed Kirchner's precept of printing it himself (which was in fact done by the Parisian master lithographer, Mourlot), he would have put each of the 1,750 sheets through the press a number of times, separately inking every colour. As it was, he wore out six pencils, signing them at a sitting to satisfy British Customs Regulations, when they arrived at the bonded warehouse in England.

If colour lithography appeals specially to the painter, etching and chalk lithography appeal to artists who like to draw a line. Matisse is said by his daughter to have seen lithography primarily as a new way of drawing; Nicolson's graphic work invariably

Oskar Kokoschka *Statue of Liberty I* 1967
Lithograph, edition 75, courtesy Marlborough Fine Art Ltd, London

opposite
Ben Nicolson *Column and Tree* 1967
Etching, edition 50, courtesy Marlborough Fine Art Ltd, London

Picasso *Vollard Suite 63* 1933
Etching, edition 303, courtesy Redfern Gallery, London

celebrates his talent for putting a sublime line round things;
while Kokoschka takes a plate with him when he goes sketching.
Picasso, commissioned by Vollard between the wars to make a
suite of a hundred etchings, demonstrated the exquisite simplicity
of an etched line (frequently finer than a pen) in a major portfolio
exploring at depth artist—model relationships and the nature of
creativity.

Picasso *Minotauromachy* 1935
Etching, edition approx. 30, courtesy London Arts

Although some of the *Vollard Suite* and many book illustrations of the 1930s display inventive techniques, and Picasso aimed to achieve blacks 'like Rembrandt' with the tissue of deeply bitten cross-hatching particularly evident in his iconographically major 1935 etching, *The Minotauromachy*, which prefigures *Guernica*, it was at the end of World War II, when he spent four months in the Mourlot atelier, that his graphic creativity knew no bounds. Working on stone, cutting up and collaging effects on transfer paper, he grew fascinated by metamorphosing an idea through as many as eighteen states. In the late 1950s and early 1960s he

Picasso
(Left) *Buste en Profil* 1957
Lithograph, edition 50
(Right) *Dame à la Collerette* 1963
Lino-cut, edition 50
Courtesy London Arts

ensured that the hitherto humble amateur's lino-cut, especially as a single block cut and printed in successive colours serially, would never look quite the same again; while in 1968 an orgiastic burst of 347 etchings and sugar aquatints made with Crommelynk at Mougins on themes from his fading virility to tales of Don Quixote, showed that whatever else was fading, invention was not. His ability to work freely in either direction, building up to black, or scratching and burnishing from black back to white, is unparalleled.

Chagall and Miro have also had great involvement with graphic media, while, his colour etchings singing like stained glass, Rouault too is a major twentieth-century printmaker.

On the question of 'originality' he provides an amusing endpiece. Vollard, impatient for Rouault to finish the *Miserere Suite*, gave him a helping hand by photo-etching the drawings, on themes of sin and regeneration, on to plates. Rouault so loathed the results, that he obliterated all but minutest traces, hand-working the magnificent fifty-eight large black and white plates with scraper, roulette, graded aquatints, file, glasspaper, and directly brushed acid. About the only thing he didn't do was dance on them wearing ice skates.

While American print lover Carl Zigrosser claims *Miserere* as 'original', Felix Man (dragging engraving into a history of lithography) said: 'With some of these large plates it seems most likely that besides aquatint, a photographic process was involved in procuring them which would make them doubtful as "original" work by the artist.'

Rouault *Clown* from *Miserere Suite* 1948
Etching and aquatint, edition 425, courtesy Redfern Gallery, London

The recent past
and the case of the non-original non-reproduction

In a half century devoted to establishing the concept of 'originality' in printmaking as synonymous with hand-work done entirely by the artist, and defining that prints not 'originals' must be termed reproductions, it was inevitable that artists, who travel too fast for definitions to keep up with them, should discover a medium neither original in this special sense, nor reproductive.

For in the past decade, the print has interested more artists than ever before, including Constructivist, Minimal, and Optical exponents, who require a non-gestural impersonal surface as far from the hand-made as possible, and Pop artists who, instead of working from life, use processed imagery which has often already been mechanically printed. Indeed, selection, re-presentation association, and transformation of printed ready-made elements has gathered momentum from the days when Cubists collaged newspapers, Max Ernst juxtaposed engravings and rubbed *frottages*, and Schwitters arranged the contents of his wastepaper basket in unique works. In our programmatic post-Duchamp world, the way has been paved for the new-wave printmaker to have an idea basically collage in concept, but to delegate its realization and editioning to a sophisticated specialist.

Richard Hamilton first found such a specialist, screen-printer Christopher Prater of Kelpra Studio, who has served the needs of artists from both sides of the Atlantic.

Hamilton, the artist who has dared most with his use of processed material in paintings and prints, is also, paradoxically, the one most fascinated by the hand-made which he continually contrasts with marks filtered through various technologies. The first print he made with Prater was *Adonis in Y Fronts* from his series *Towards a Definitive Statement on the Coming Trends in Menswear and Accessories.* Utilizing both hand-cut and photographic screens, the print unites advertisements for vodka and underwear from *Playboy*, trims the hero's contours to match the Hermes of Praxiteles and muscle-men, and obtains a beautiful

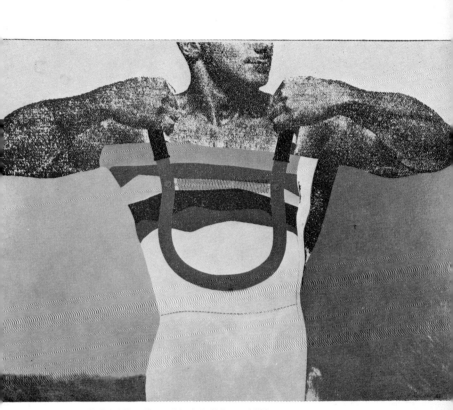

Richard Hamilton *Adonis in Y Fronts* 1963
Screenprint, edition 40, courtesy Victoria and Albert Museum, London
Crown copyright reserved

dragged quality in the background by four different shades of
silver, each worked direct on the screen. It took eighteen separate
inkings to obtain the qualities Hamilton wanted. After printing
an edition of forty, he tried to interest Marlborough Fine Art, and
failing, sold twenty copies to friends at £4 apiece, to cover his
printing costs. Those interested in market values will be fascinated
to know that Prater has since turned down an offer of £600 for
his copy.

Paolozzi was another artist early on the Kelpra screenprinting scene, and *Metalization of a Dream* is related to early sculptures in which *objets trouvés* from various sources are integrated through a technical process. Studying Surrealist documents in France, Paolozzi noticed how tatty and brown mass media collages became. This drawback to unique collage is overcome by screenprinting, for completely disparate imagery can be smoothly unified. Paolozzi achieved the medium's first masterpiece with his brilliant *As is When* portfolio (page 59) based on the life and writings of the philosopher Ludwig Wittgenstein. The series integrated elements from various visual languages— crochet patterns, engineering diagrams, Woolworth's papers—and even went on giving birth to itself when spoils from an earlier sheet in the series were collaged into *Wittgenstein the Soldier*. Paolozzi has written that screenprinting provided him with a complexity and range of possibility inaccessible to normal art or craft printers. Ignoring the usual craft maxim that each print in an edition should be identical, he worked out a permutation of eighty-eight colourways to ensure that each print in his edition was unique.

The screenprints of Patrick Caulfield present a particularly interesting case, simply because the artist makes full-scale gouaches of the images to be printed, so that if one wants to apply the word 'reproductive' it is in some ways legitimate. The acid test, however, is that the master is intended for print, and since Caulfield's style resembles the bland black-edged anonymous images often found in children's painting books, it is ideal for screenprinting and might have been designed to facilitate registration. In his paintings, aesthetic transmutations of the banal, he works out imagery too large for the conventional print scale, yet theoretically only market considerations prevent these images too from being screenprinted and editioned. Caulfield says he would always need to paint an image first to have absolute control over it; after that it is a fascinating proposition that such is the overlap between art-forms, the only differences between a painting and a print might be whether it is screened on to canvas or paper, and whether it is unique or repeated.

Eduardo Paolozzi *Metalization of a Dream* 1963
Screenprint, edition 40, courtesy Editions Alecto, London

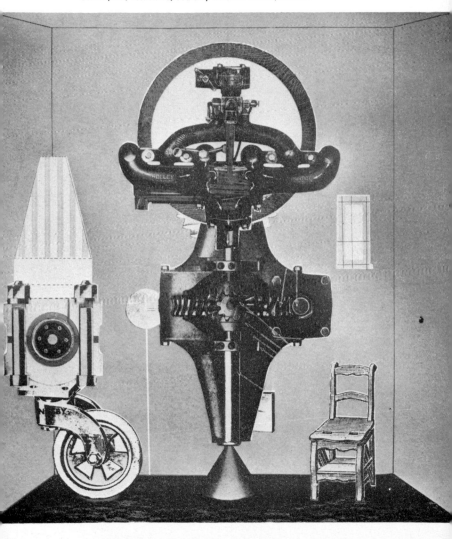

Patrick Caulfield, *Coloured Still Life* 1966
Screenprint, edition 77, courtesy Editions Alecto, London

When Caulfield's prints were shown at the Parisian Biennale de Jeunes in 1965 together with others from a set of two dozen published by the Institute of Contemporary Arts in London, an official insisted first on their disqualification, then that they should be segregated from the hand-done prints because they were not 'originals'. Caulfield nevertheless won an award from the Biennale—the privilege of exhibiting again two years later.

As long ago as 1922, Moholy Nagy ordered paintings over the telephone to be made by a sign factory whose representative noted specifications on a square grid and colour chart. Images like Vasarely's *Permutation 8*, *Bolgar* (page 58), simple in basic form, yet incredibly complex in the way it juggles colour and suggests space, could, theoretically, be created similarly. In various manifestos Vasarely has spoken not of originals but of prototypes, which he intends to be re-created without preferential scale or technique. Their value, he says, lies in rarity of quality, not rarity of object, and without denying the principle of uniqueness, he finds multiplicity 'more generous, and more human'. Conceiving and causing to be done, rather than feeling and doing, is, he maintains, in harmony with technical civilization and scientific discovery, and he writes:

The aestheticising and literary world, under the cloak of the human and the sensitive, wages its battle against the new, and proscribes the use of the conquests of technique in art. . . . The stone cutter, the weaver, the mosaicist, make way for the helio engraver, the camera-man, the master printer. Let us not be waylaid in the matter of ends and means The tool is the prolonga tion of the hand, the machine of the tool. . . .

Of all the artists who have worked with Prater in the past six years, Kitaj, the American who had to be cajoled by fellow artists to make his first screenprint, and has since outstripped them, has perhaps demanded most. *The Defects of its Qualities* won Kitaj a major award at the Bradford Print Biennale in 1968. Although he says he conceived this image primarily in the aesthetic terms of an abstraction, it perfectly sums up the complexity of print. A printed magazine photograph of Picasso is juxtaposed with a paragraph in print about Braque, whose printed signature lies above a print wrapping paper next to a printed registration form for a prostitute. This jostles the title page from the Print Council of America's guidance booklet *What is an Original Print?*

No original work of art exists from which this print has been copied. It has been conceived in the medium of execution by arranging fragments originally quite different in colour and scale associated only in the artist's mind. Kitaj did none of the work by hand: Prater's technicians made both hand-cut and photo-mechanical stencils upon verbal and handwritten direction.

The Print Council of America said in 1961 that to qualify as an 'original' print the artist must have created the master image alone; the French National Committee on Engraving in 1964 ruled out any and all mechanical or photomechanical processes in the making of an 'original' print; the Congress of Plastic Arts held in Vienna in 1960 decreed that 'original' graphics must be signed and serially numbered, and that if the artist did not himself make the plate, block, or screen, the print must be considered a reproduction.

The only thing none of these definitions explained, was, a reproduction of what?

Ron Kitaj *The Defects of its Qualities* 1967
Screenprint and collage, edition 70, courtesy Marlborough Fine Art Ltd, London

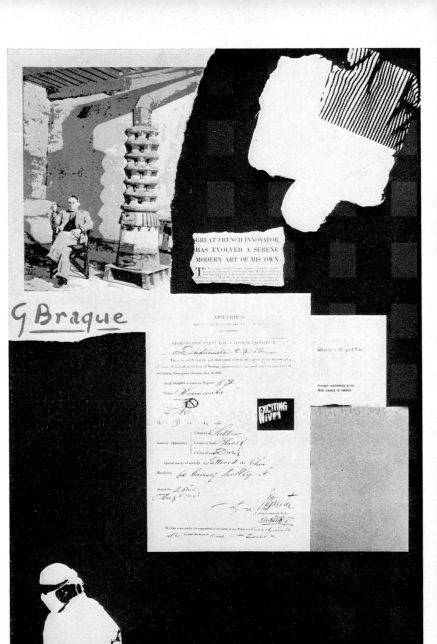

DEVELOPMENTS IN TECHNIQUE

In addition to screenprinting, the last forty years have brought more technical innovation to the three basic processes than all previous centuries. This expansion of techniques in all media has arisen partly from the artist investigating his means as never before (in which, to borrow a McLuhanism, the medium becomes the message), and partly from the development of 'originality' causing the artist to work out his ideas in the language of print itself, valuing the idiosyncratic features to be won by his tools from wood, metal, or stone. Many twentieth-century printmakers would agree with the American Gabor Peterdi, that even if single examples only could be pulled, they would nevertheless make them to achieve effects otherwise unobtainable.

A dichotomy to some extent exists between the full-time craft specialist, and the artist famous for painting or sculpture, encouraged by his dealer to widen his market, yet regarding printmaking as a minor, subsidiary activity. It has been said that while craftsmen laboriously uncover techniques, only great masters can take advantage of them. Certainly many a craftsman can bite a plate fifty-seven different ways and say nothing, but conversely few internationally renowned artists have made significant prints by mere dabbling. Picasso, Miro, Chagall, primarily painters, have geared their ideas superbly to autographic media realizing how to exploit their unique potential, as have younger generations including Rauschenberg, Allen Jones, Jim Dine, and Jasper Johns; the feat is equally possible when Kitaj and Paolozzi unite concept and means employing craftsmen and photo-process. The crux of the problem for any printmaker, is to make a statement using the specific qualities of the chosen graphic medium. If the statement is interesting enough, the print can be a major vehicle of expression; its bonus is that, existing in many examples, it may have a wider circulation than a unique work.

It has in the past been easier, however, art market *status quo* and the prestige of the unique being what it is, for the artist established in another field to find a notable niche in print, than for the specialist printmaker to win international laurels.

Gertrude Hermes *The Ram* 1958
Woodcut and lino-cut, edition 50, courtesy Robert Erskine

Relief printing

The earliest relief material used was wood, and in the first woodcuts a drawing pasted to a block was knife-cut to print as a
raised line. Coarseness of plank grain caused eighteenth-century
printmakers to switch to end-grain wood capable of finer tooling
with a burin, and this degenerated in the nineteenth century into
the lifeless reproductive medium Gauguin reacted against.

In a work such as *The Ram*, by Gertrude Hermes, who helped
set free the English relief print from book illustration, one can
see a mixture of influences: plank grain, bold revitalized gouging,
as well as delicate white line work.

Klaus Menzel *no. II/68* 1968
Woodcut, courtesy Xylon, Switzerland

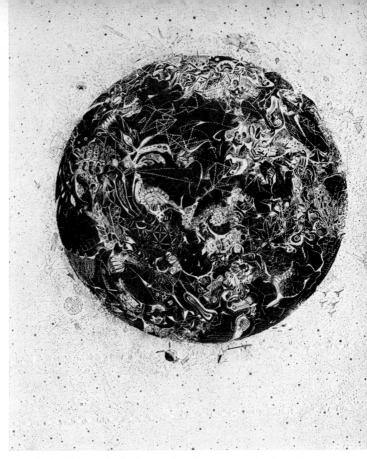

Josef Gielniak *Improvisation-Lucubration-Humorous and Fanciful* 1964
Lino-cut, courtesy Grabowski Gallery, London

Virtuosity in wood tooling is demonstrated in the black and
white prizewinning print of Xylon 1969, by the German Klaus
Menzel, whose technical repertoire includes power tools, milling,
drilling, filing, hammered wire gauzes, and wire brushing, to
obtain the nuances he loves. On the other hand, a craftsman such
as the Pole Josef Gielniak, who spends much time in a sanatorium,
can ply traditional engraving tools and achieve, on lino, a crumbly
material generally given coarser treatment, the fragility of dew
on a spider's web in the fairy-tale pen illustrations of Jessie M.
King.

Louis Schanker *Dance* 1948
Ten colour woodcut, unlimited edition

Leonard Baskin *The Angel of Death* 1959
Woodcut, unlimited edition

The Americans, on whom Oriental and German Expressionist influence has been far-reaching, have taken to woodcutting, and Frasconi, Misch Kohn, who wields a multiple tool with cunning, and Leonard Baskin, whose work ranges from tiny vignettes to huge man-high unlimited edition woodcuts like *The Angel of Death*, exhibited at the Venice Biennale in 1968, have achieved world fame.

In her essay on the decade of US printmaking, 1947–56, Una Johnson of Brooklyn Museum noted that expansion in size and colour had enabled prints (a polyptych by Adja Yunkers 14 feet × 3 feet 8 in. employing fifty-six colours, for example) to vie with paintings or even murals. Pioneer work was done within the Graphic Arts Division of the Works Progress Administration in the late 1930s, when Louis Schanker developed wet-on-wet colour printing in rhythmic abstractions and achieved new effects of transparency; his legacy can be traced to his pupil, Carol

Ed Casarella, one of six paper relief plates for *Tree Burst* 1954

Summers. The beautiful blurred effects Summers obtains in his transformations of landscape, such as *Fontelimon* (page 94), are made by putting a Japanese paper over shapes gouged from plywood and inking on top of it, occasionally spraying ink thinner afterwards to diffuse the soft colour yet further.

It occurred to Ed Casarella in 1949 that paper could as well form a printing surface as wood. 'If you can ink it, you can print it,' is a dictum he likes. He also discarded the one-colour-one-block

Ed Casarella *Tree Burst* 1954
Paper relief cut

idea. By printing as many as sixty colours with as few as six paper plates, as in *Tree Burst,* he claims he invaded painting's territory with a legitimate print. Although dolly colour printing (inking up separated areas of one block with different shades) has a long history in intaglio, it has not been widely used in relief. Derain attacked the problem by cutting a white line to isolate each colour, while Munch would divide up his wood-blocks for inking and reassemble them in the press.

Such division is not problematic when the print has been liberated from the tyranny of the rectangle—a contribution from Michael Rothenstein, said to have had as stimulating an effect on relief as Hayter on intaglio. Using an open block-printing method allows him to combine on the press-bed 'wild' materials (found objects such as driftwood planks, intriguing metal scrap) with processed blocks, as well as hand-cut elements, particularly the large calligraphic gestures interpreted in gouged lino, for a long time his hallmark. Such is the finesse and importance to the final work of his printing, that he cannot delegate it to others. *Liquitio* celebrates a discovery made by the accidental spilling of cooker cleaner, that caustic will etch and lower a lino block's surface, producing almost painterly tonal gradation.

Intaglio

In traditional intaglio—inking the indentations in a metal plate, and wiping its surface before printing—it is possible to make marks by cutting directly into the metal, or by removing a protective ground with a needle before placing it in an acid bath so grooves can be bitten, or etched.

Michael Rothenstein *Liquitio* 1962
Etched and engraved lino, edition 35

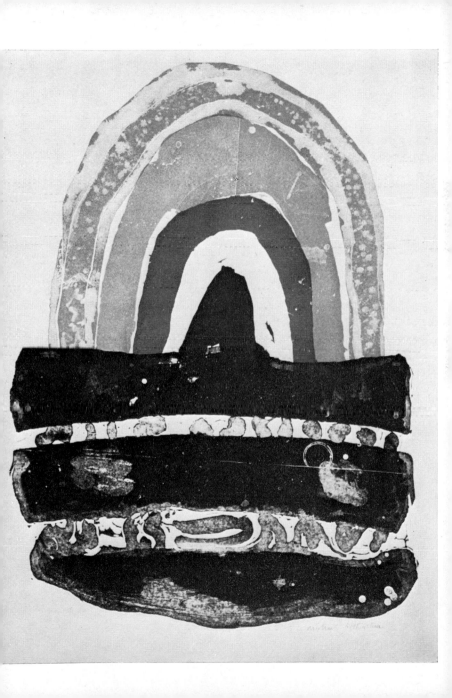

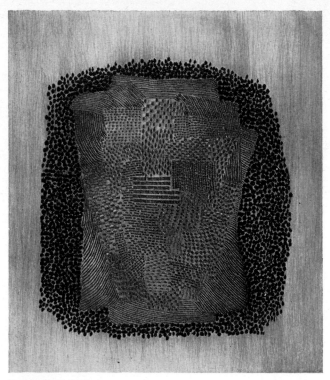

Piza *Pyramide* 1964
Gouge gravure, edition 50, courtesy La Hune, Paris

Direct marks can be made by drypoint, which prints a furred ink bleed from a burr, shortlived because easily crushed in the press, and by burin which goes ahead of the hand as the plate is swivelled to direct the clean dynamic cut. Typically twentieth-century use of direct cutting has been made by Piza, for whom various gouge jabs determine the print, while the French sculptor Henri-Georges Adam, significantly also a tapestry designer and honoured in 1957 by grand prizes both at Tokyo and Ljubljana Print Biennales, creates tissues of burin-engraved filaments forming spatial nets in cutout shapes. The Swede Karl Häggblad attacks the plate with an oxyacetylene gas-welding torch, making caves, holes, and ridges of molten metal, attracting vestiges of ink.

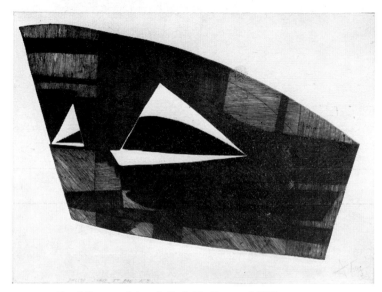

Henri-Georges Adam *Dalle, Sable, Eaux no. 3* 1956
Burin engraving, edition 50, courtesy La Hune, Paris

Karl Erik Häggblad *Droppas I relief* 1965
Gas-welded metal, edition 30

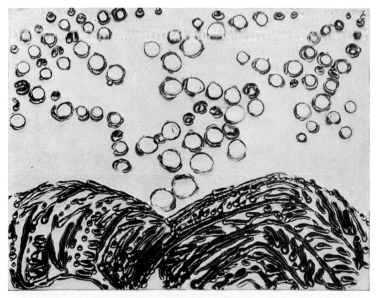

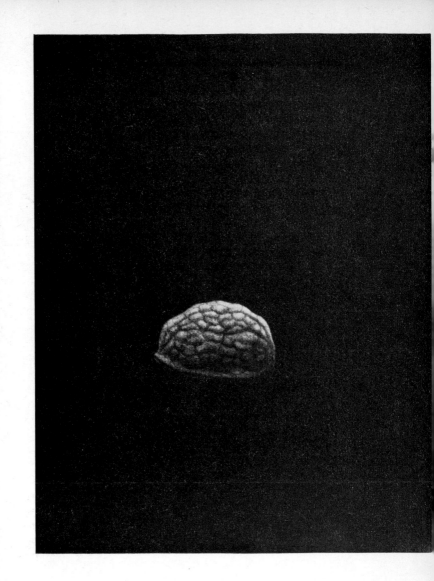

Hamaguchi *Walnut c.* 1960
Mezzotint, edition 60, courtesy Lumley Cazalet Ltd, London

Merlyn Evans *Diptych* 1963
Mezzotint, edition 75

A laborious method for obtaining tone directly is mezzotinting, made by working the metal in every conceivable direction with a curved serrated rocker which pits the plate minutely until a sheet would print a matt black velvet. Purists like Avati, who works his copper in sixty directions to a background of classical music, maintain no black equals it, and burnishing must win back whites and greys by complete or relative smoothing of the roughness. The Japanese Hamaguchi has made the method, once primarily reproductive, very much his own, with contemplative still lives such as the mysterious planetary *Walnut*, while Merlyn Evans has given it an entirely modern slant in bold abstract forms like *Diptych*, in which blacks contrast some areas rocked partially to make cellular and striated greys.

Anthony Gross *Study of Trees no. 1* 1961
Demonstration etched plate for Victoria and Albert Museum, London
Crown copyright reserved

Soulages *Composition* 1958
Etching, edition 100, courtesy Gimpel Fils, London

Gross, who made the demonstration plate *Trees* for the Victoria
and Albert Museum, London, shows the versatile tooling and
stippling obtainable with etching. The customary needle is not
pushed, like the burin, but moved back and forth as is a pencil,
and can be accompanied by multiple points, the tiny teeth of the
roulette or even an ornamental doorknob for broad patterns.
Intensity can be varied by protecting it from acid early in fine
areas, and allowing deeper biting for darkness, or by burnishing
afterwards: all intaglio marks are to some extent reversible, and
can be partly polished from the plate.

In the deep-etched scarred work of Soulages, the acid is
allowed to erode the rectangle and the form, not preconceived,
is born of the 'combat de l'acide contre la cuivre'.

Bartolomeu dos Santos *Portuguese Men-of-War* 1961
Aquatint, edition 50, courtesy London Arts

Bartolomeu dos Santos, a Portuguese who teaches with Gross
at the Slade School, London, shows in *Portuguese Men-of-War*,
a ship-o'-fools from the Establishment, an unusually pure use of
aquatint, generally teamed with etched line. To aquatint, the
plate is heat-fused with a fine resin powder giving a porous
resist which bites as a tone. Whites can be stopped out initially,
while a range of greys can be achieved by progressive immersions
in acid, until only those areas to print black are exposed in the
final bath.

It is characteristic of intaglio, which leaves a pressure mark in
the paper, that what is cut or bitten deepest within the plate will

Rolf Nesch *Pegasus* 1968
Etching, 12 variations

be raised highest above the paper, but the metal prints of the
naturalized Norwegian Rolf Nesch have a palpable tactile
effect. Nesch found in 1925 that an accidentally bitten hole made
a bubble in the paper, and he followed the discovery by adding to
his intaglio plates, soldered wires, meshes, movable sheets of
punched zinc, washers, and so on. Variously inked, such plates
are sculpturally impressed into heavy paper, and having created
monumental mural print groupings, centred on themes such as
herring fishing and reindeer massacre in the country of his adop-
tion, the media themselves are assembled as material pictures.

Michael Ponce de Leòn *Succubus* 1968
Collage intaglio, edition 10

Stanley William Hayter *Famille Japonaise* 1955
Soft ground etching and engraving, edition 100, courtesy Editions
Alecto, London

Carried to a kind of super-American extreme, the collage-
intaglios of Michael Ponce de Leòn aim to 'avoid facility'. His
work *Succubus* began with a carved shape which he cast, then
aquatinted as an aluminium matrix to print a three-dimensional
spiral of twenty-eight colours. This was mounted on a background bas-relief imprinted by a perforated sewer-drain cover
plus metals etched and welded on a zinc plate. To produce each
print was a five-hour operation utilizing custom-built mould-
shaped paper, in which one of the ingredients was linen from
his brother's underpants, hand-made inks, and a hydraulic press
of his own invention exerting a force of 10,000 lb; that kind of
determination gets a nation to the moon.

British-born S. W. Hayter, scientifically trained, has made the
greatest technical discoveries and innovations, developing new

means of expression in what Herbert Read called the 'Cinderella of the Arts which had never previously realized half its potential'. Starting the famous group workshop Atelier 17 in Paris in 1927, operating in America during World War II, and returning to France after it, Hayter has not only given such artists as Picasso and Miro technical advice but has left the imprint of his powerful personality on successive generations of students from across the world. Notable himself for burin bravura, and the textural device of natural and woven materials pressed into a soft ground and etched, as in *Famille Japonaise,* his most far-reaching contribution, which developed from printing intaglio and relief simultaneously from one plate, has been in the realm of colour printing. He has pioneered the use of different viscosities at different depths, selectively depositing inks by using hard and soft rollers (which ride over ridges, or sink into hollows) as well as by stencilling or off-setting colour on to controlled areas. The one-plate technique has overcome the major difficulty of intaglio colour printing, that of accurately registering successive plates on a sheet which can shrink when dampened for printing.

One of Hayter's most recent students, who won a French Government scholarship enabling him to travel to Paris, is the twenty-four-year-old Malaysian Long Thien Shih. His distinctive deep-etched multipartite plate, *Last Day of 1968*, with curling abstractions possibly inspired by ancient Chinese metal ware, is based on a love-making scene and ably demonstrates Hayter's most significant discovery (page 58).

This principle, of inking a plate both in its deep-etched intaglio, and on its flat relief surface, blurs the division between two hitherto distinct printmaking categories, and in some ways makes nonsense of technical definitions. Fiorini has even made such prints from plywood, gouging out layers to several different depths, and glossing parts of the relief with paint. Fusion of intaglio and relief is particularly evident in the use of man-made substances such as plastics. They have inspired much experimentation in the New World. Arthur Deshaies, who has engraved plexiglass and lucite, both for relief and intaglio printing, finds the

Deshaies *Hornets Nest* 1956
Engraving on lucite, courtesy Victoria and Albert Museum, London
Crown copyright reserved

Page 58
(Top) **Vasarely** *Permutation 8: Bolgar* 1968
Screenprint, edition 150, courtesy London Arts

(Bottom) **Long Thien Shih** *Last Day of 1968*
Etching, edition 40, courtesy Curwen Gallery, London

Eduardo Paolozzi *As is When: Wittgenstein the Soldier* 1965
Screenprint, edition 65, courtesy Editions Alecto, London

transparency of plastic an advantage in that it allows taped preparatory drawings underneath while cutting; Boris Margo invented the *Cellocut*, building images with plastic dissolved in acetone on a rigid support, dripping the liquid in layers, texturing and working it, and printing relief, intaglio, or both, with soft, sometimes almost rubbery effects.

Werner Schreib *Black Whisky Moon of Alabama* 1966
Plastic intaglio, edition 50

James Guitet *Gravure 55* 1966
Textigravure, edition 65

Not only Americans have put plastic to work. James Guitet of France, who won engraving prizes at Venice in 1962 and Ljubljana in 1963, has devised a method of using it to 'fossilize' natural objects such as leaves and eggshells, together with woven materials. He calls such 'reveries de la matière' *Taxti gravures,* creates an imaginary geology in an imaginary space, and prints with an etching press, austerely using black and white in the belief of so many graphic artists that these two contain absolute shadow and the purest light: 'Graver, c'est mettre le mystère des ombres de l'encre sur la lumière d'un beau papier.' (To engrave is to put the mystery of the shadows of ink on the light of a beautiful paper.)

The German Werner Schreib, coating a metal plate with a malleable polyester paste mixed with ground quartzite which hardens after twenty-four hours, uses spatulas to mould ridges and serial structures, and presses in various *objets trouvés* like seals, such as the bottle top in the poetic fantasy, *Black Whisky Moon of Alabama.* Such plates can be tellingly printed in one operation using different colours at various levels; it's interesting that Schreib makes unique works similarly, moulding his materials on a grander scale.

Étienne Hajdu *Estampille: Tête au Chapeau* 1965
Artist's proof, inkless embossing
64

Marjan Pogačnik *Unseen by the Roadside* 1967 (detail)
Intaglio, courtesy Ljubljana Biennale

Another form of printing achieved by both relief and intaglio methods is inkless embossing, in which the relief in the paper can be conceived as pure form, white on white. Working at Hayter's atelier, the Hungarian sculptor Etienne Hajdu cut out zinc shapes, arranged them on the printing bed and compressed them into damp paper, so that the stretched white created a smooth relief against the roughness of the original sheet—a graphic equivalent for his work in marble. Yugoslav artist Marjan Pogačnik creates impeccable prints embodying symbolic sign systems in relief, this 1967 example suggesting the wayside tragedies caused by life's speed. The white relief in the paper has been moulded from deep-etched hollows in a metal plate, the surface of which was protected by asphaltum during biting; some inking contributes cream, porridge, brown, and black areas to emphasize the paper's relief whiteness. (See frontispiece.)

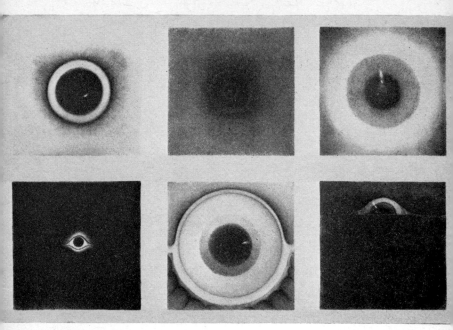

Rodolfo Abularach *Eye Series no. 2* 1967
Lithograph, edition 10, courtesy Bradford Biennale

Lithography

As discovered in 1798 by Senefelder, lithography consisted of drawing with waxy materials on a grained limestone. This technique has since extended to special metal or plastic plates. The wax can be applied by fine stick—the hypnotic *Eye Series no. 2* by the Guatemalan Rodolfo Abularach showing how sensitive such pencil technique can be—by coarse crayon, by liquid tusche on pen or brush, and by splash and splatter. On stone, the dark can be illuminated by scratching away the wax with blades, points, or glasspaper, a procedure brought to a pinnacle by Odilon Redon in the nineteenth century, and much copied. Washes, known as *lavis*, can be made by thinning tusche with various solvents—distilled water, petrol, turpentine—which dry out sometimes forming globular drifts, sometimes with a

Ceri Richards *And Death Shall Have No Dominion* 1965
Lithograph, edition 70, courtesy Marlborough Fine Art Ltd, London

gentle shirring like the delicate withdrawing eddies of an ebb
tide. An anti-machine conspiracy maintains that the subtle
alchemy of *lavis* can only be obtained on stone. It isn't true: the
Curwen Press (London) lithographer, Stanley Jones, knows how
to procure and maintain it on plates, the most fugitive washes
unimpaired for perhaps three hundred impressions, robust ones
lasting longer.

Drawings or rubbed textures on special paper can be transferred
to the lithographic surface (conveniently reversing an image for
correct printing) and the tribute to the Welsh poet Dylan Thomas,
And Death Shall Have No Dominion, shows crayoning, painted
and thumbed tusche, transferred impressions rubbed from
corrugated card and a cut-glass motif, beautifully assembled for

67

Shmuel Shapiro *Dying Mother and Child* 1967
Lithograph, edition 75, courtesy Maltzahn Gallery, London

Alan Davie *Zurich Improvisations nos. 1 and 8* 1965
Lithographs, edition 25 each, courtesy Gimpel Fils, London

the magnificent black and white image by Ceri Richards. Shapiro,
in his moving Jewish suite concerning the systematic slaughter
of a race, monoprinted tusche on to the stone, drawing the
smeary furred line through a sheet of transfer paper coated with it.

Once the greasy image is chemically fixed the print can be
made, because ink rolled on to it has an affinity for grease, but is
repelled by the dampened stone. Colours must be printed one by
one on the paper with a registered plate or stone for each, unless
two colours are far enough apart on it to be separately inked.
This premeditated process is not well suited, on the face of it, to
the spontaneity of the Abstract Expressionist, but Alan Davie,
who began with the intention of making three prints, each with
five plates, discovered that he could permutate them endlessly
with unexpected outcome. The result was *Zurich Improvisations*
and Paul Cornwall Jones (the founder of Editions Alecto and the
Petersburg Press in London) tells how a fantastic web of proofs

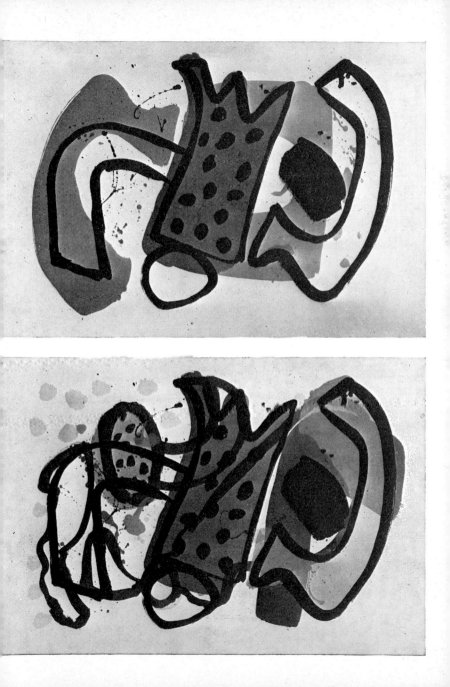

spread around the studios as the printers frantically turned Davie's programmes into fact, and, caught up in the communal excitement, began making improvisations themselves.

No-one has used colour more breathtakingly than Chagall, whose plates for the *belle-livre Daphnis and Chloe*, separately editioned (page 95), were declared by the printer Mourlot his most important graphic work. Using various crayon and brush-weights in each colour, and sumptuous effects in wash, Chagall worked three years on the undertaking—a pastoral love story lyrically interpreted.

Andrew Stasik, the director of the Pratt Graphics Center in New York, features a lithographic wash for the aquamarine background of *Summer XXXVI*, atmospherically surrounding a schematic house, bottle, and flowers in hand-drawn serigraphy, contrasting ink translucency and opacity by combining media.

Screenprinting

Serigraphy (silk-drawing) is a word coined in America as an attempt to differentiate artist's prints from the crude commercial silkscreen process for supermarket price tags. In fact, silk has already had its day, and the synthetic meshes widely used probably make screenprinting, as Prater prefers to call it, a more accurate terminology.

The simplest use of the method is by hand-cut paper stencils blocking parts of a gauze stretched on a wooden frame. The unblocked mesh permits colour, passed over the screen with a rubber blade inside the frame, to coat the paper beneath. The result has none of the sensuous varying tonal quality of a lithographic mark, but deposits a rich, even ink layer. Drawn or tonal marks can be achieved by brushing or texture rubbing on to the screen in a grease which repels the water-based glue applied to

Andrew Stasik *Summer XXXVI* 1968
Screenprint and lithograph, edition 31

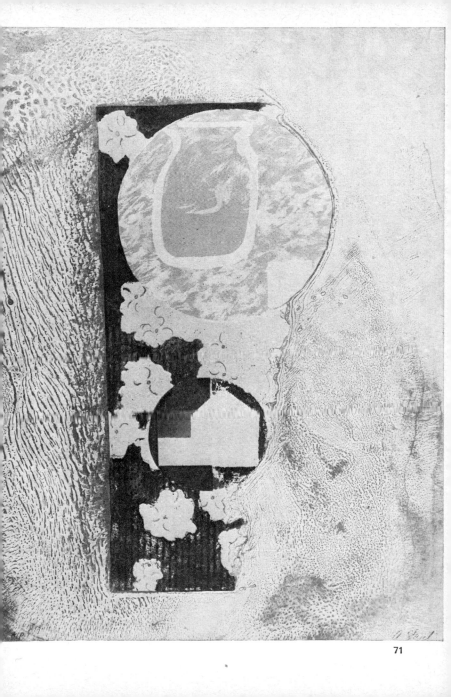

Anthony Velonis *Side Street* 1940
Screenprint, courtesy Brooklyn Museum, NY

block the rest of the pores. When this has dried, the original marks are dissolved, opening their mesh, but leaving the glue, resistant to oil inks, intact to form a stencil. Anthony Velonis, whose *Side Street* was done in this way, was one of the pioneers of the method in America in the late 1930s.

Where an artist's gesture is required in the work, he must fashion his own screen. Lithography gives such an artist greater scope, and confirmed lithographers are rarely as confident in screen-printing. But when the style of work is a geometrical abstraction, or requires a machine finish—as does that of Vasarely and other hard-edge artists—the insistence on 'original' autography be-

Richard Smith *Cigarettes* 1964
Screenprint, edition 40, courtesy ICA, London

comes meaningless. When an artist goes further and requires in his work the hitherto commercial and infinitely complex process of trichromatic half-tones, or polarization and posterization of images, only the help of a master-craftsman with the necessary expensive technological equipment will enable him to achieve them.

The English Institute of Contemporary Arts project in 1963/64 which cemented Prater's decision to abandon commercial work and become a fine art printer, introduced two dozen artists to screenprinting, including Richard Smith, whose interest in packaging and illusory space was neatly interpreted by the cigarette pack four times magnified. But the rapport which must

73

exist between artist and printer perhaps developed most profound-
ly between Prater and Ron Kitaj. Explaining once that he wished
to do Cézanne again after Surrealism, Kitaj constructs prints,
allusive riddles with fragments both from learned books and
urban ephemera, to create a visual poetry hinting at the complex
layers of experience. Figurative elements susceptible to lengthy
decoding can thus be woven into a pictorial fabric which can
also be relatively swiftly read as an abstraction. *The Good Old
Days*, from the portfolio *The Struggle in the West* inspired by
London's war-time, frames a chequerboard of images redolent of
force, helplessness, and destruction, with zebra skin cornerstones,
two underlining dole queues, and wallpapers which evoke for
Kitaj the flavour of the period. Technically the print is one of the
most demanding on which Prater has collaborated, running
through five states of constantly adjusted proofs, its formidable
editioning involving forty-three printings on the main sheet, and
the collaging of six pieces requiring thirteen printings, as well as
four varnished shapes—a total of eighty-one operations in all.
The 'original' print enthusiast, claiming an artist who does not
actually manipulate his own materials cannot realize their
potential, could perhaps make a reassessment on this evidence.

Ron Kitaj *The Good Old Days* 1969
Screenprint and collage from *The Struggle in the West*, edition 70, courtesy
Marlborough Fine Art Ltd, London

Die gute alte Zeit

PHOTOGRAPHY AND THE MACHINE

When Landseer's brother referred to the 'foe-to-graphic art', his pun summed up a fear of photography felt not only by hand copyists made redundant by photo-process but by artists everywhere, who either regarded machines as threats, or if they used them as accomplices, did not advertise their debt.

As Aaron Scharf suggested, the *cliché verre*, a print technique practised by Corot, in which opaquely coated glass is hand-scratched providing a negative to contact-print light-sensitive paper, but for the stigma attached to photographic process in relation to art, might have become an important means of expression.

As it was, the nineteenth century abounded in artistic/reproductive wrangles, printmakers such as Pennell attacking Professor Herkomer for wrongfully describing as etchings plates which *had* been etched but from his drawings transferred to sensitized metal by light, then stoutly defending himself when Sickert claimed that his transferred lithographs did not compare, and should not be classified, with those direct from stone. Almost hysterical arguments were advanced to separate the inseparable, forgetting that in the realm of printing the most autographic needs a 'tool' (sometimes cousin to that stamping out car-body panels) and a machine, the press, while the most mechanical process needs a sensitive retouching hand, and colour-correcting eye. 'The false distinction,' as Gray wisely observed in *The English Print*, 'is not in the process, but in the way in which, and the purpose for which it is used.'

Although artists have gradually pushed aside constrictions concerning photographic and mechanical processes, that nineteenth-century attitudes to them were firmly entrenched in the late 1950s is evidenced by the Parisian *Maeght Editeur* catalogue, reviewing, by illustration, ten years of 'original' printing from 1946 to 1956. In this M. Georges Limbour apologized with irony that: 'Il est composé de ce dont la Maison a particulière-ment en horreur: de reproductions mécaniques, de reflets photographiques!' (It is composed of that which this House finds particularly horrific: mechanical reproductions, reflections of photography!)

Allen Jones *Runnymede, Wapping—Windsor* suite 1960
Offset litho, edition 70, courtesy Robert Erskine

Mechanics of lithography

'Originality' not only outlawed the photographic transfer of images to the printing surface but also queried even hand-drawn plates if printed by a commercial quantity—production process such as offset lithography, in which automatic inking, and a rubber-blanketed roller intervening between plate and paper, 'offset' the image.

When Robert Erskine, the pioneering English post-war publisher, produced the series *Wapping—Windsor* by this method in 1960, including Allen Jones's *Runnymede*, he took pains to educate people to the technical departure. Although he hardly needed to justify a 'down-to-earth process used for printing beer-bottle labels' which enabled him to sell prints from a limited edition of seventy for £3 10s each, the artists nevertheless did not pencil sign or number their sheets.

Karin Székessy photo 1968
Courtesy Brusberg Gallery, Hanover, Skékessy

Jim Dine *Cincinnati, I* 1969
Offset litho, edition 75, courtesy Petersburg Press, London

Paul Wunderlich *Lithograph no. 209 1000*
Edition 75, courtesy Brusberg Gallery, Hanover

More recently, changing attitudes allowed the same process to
be used with less diffidence in the intense tripled black of Jim
Dine's hand-drawn offset lithograph *Cincinnati I*, repeatedly
driven home with deadly precision.

Photography is often naïvely written about as if it had no more
than documentary power, the chronicling of fact. If so, German
lithographer Paul Wunderlich knows fact can be stranger than
fiction. He collaborates with photographer Karin Székessy who
drapes models tellingly against the eccentric mannerist contents
of his flat, while Wunderlich translates her mysterious effects
even more eerily into lithography by hand, sometimes helped
by an epidiascope. Brusberg Gallery are editioning their works
together.

John Piper *Bethesda Chapel* 1966
Photo-litho, edition 75, courtesy Marlborough Fine Art, London

As with screenprinting, only an artist with access to technical
assistants and machinery can take advantage of the complexity
of new developments in industrial lithography. In America such
work has been initiated by Eugene Feldman; in Great Britain,
Stanley Jones at the Curwen Studio helped John Piper in 1964
with photo-litho techniques in one image from the *Retrospect of
Churches*. Piper found intervening to reduce or intensify the
photograph, together with hand-drawn elements, extended the
mark-making possibilities, and two years later he developed a

Geoffrey Ireland *Sagres* 1965
Crystograph, unlimited edition, courtesy Curwen Gallery, London

whole set of churches along these lines, including *Bethesda Chapel*.

Curwen also published, in one of their unlimited editions, Geoffrey Ireland's *Sagres*. Working from a colour transparency of interacting chemicals, he employed an electronic colour scanner called a Vario-Klischograph, which engraves the tri-chromatic separations usual in commercial colour printing on to plastic; it awaits further development by a technologically orientated artist.

The intriguing images of Austrian Hans Glauber are achieved entirely photographically, but editioned by lithography at Grafica Uno in Milan using barium-surfaced paper. A sociologist with Olivetti, Glauber expresses his systemic interests in art by photographing the internal arrangements of intricate mechanisms, solarizing and reversing the images to obtain a nervous black line, as in *Lithograph 7, 1965*, which he retouches or edits, and rephotographs, sometimes overlapping images to achieve symmetry, or serial repetitions with barely perceptible variations. His *Mechanical City* is thus organized by making a new formal logic out of the functional.

The competitive arena

Naturally enough, the first Print Biennales set out firmly wedded to official definitions of 'originality'—so much so, that writing of the Ljubljana Biennale in *Quadrum*, J. Leymarie congratulated the organizers for perpetuating craft traditions in an increasingly mechanized society and eliminating hybrid editions not directly from the hand of the artist. Thus, since he preaches a machine aesthetic, Vasarely's grand prize in Yugoslavia two Biennales later for screenprints which can be cut and editioned by other hands, reflected more permissive attitudes.

Hans Glauber *Lithograph no. 7* 1965
Photo-litho, edition 50

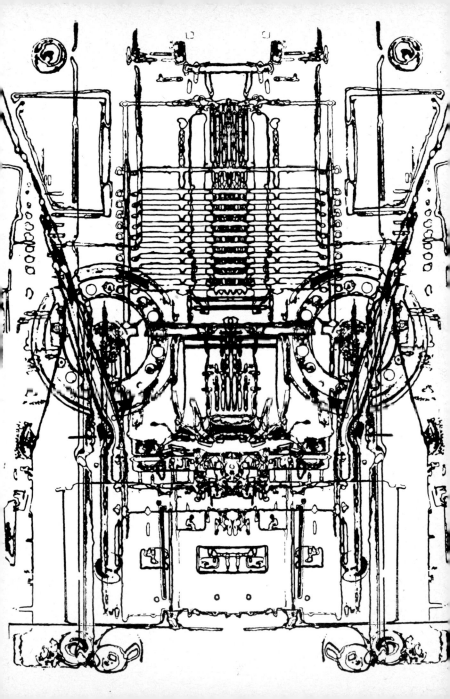

Luca Patella *Si fa cosi* 1969
Photo-etching

Lucjan Mianowski *Tête-Disque* 1968
Photo-litho, courtesy Ljubljana Biennale

Since then, photographically aided images have crept in slowly: the Italian Luca Patella, with photographic etchings, printed in simultaneous colours, like *Si fa cosi*; Lucjan Mianowski of Poland, haunted by the photo of a face which disintegrates under drops of rain, is scratched by a disc, or lithographically

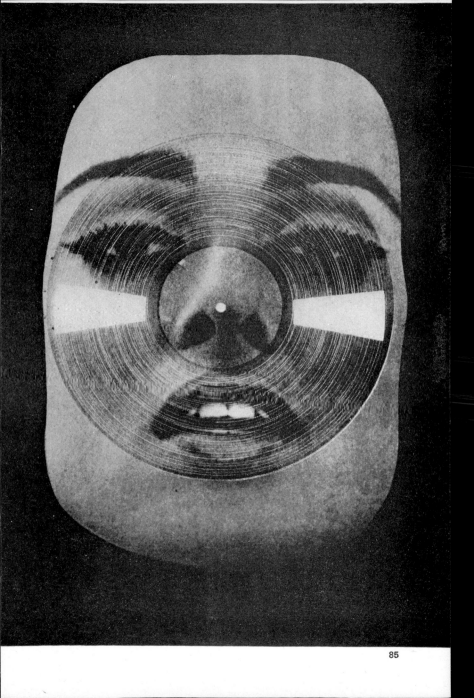

Tetsuya Noda *Diary August 22, 1968*
Woodcut and screenprint, grand prizewinner Tokyo Biennale, 1968

Julian Santamaria *Mia Figlia Raquel* 1968
Photo-litho and embossing, courtesy Venice Biennale

doubled out of register; Spaniard Julian Santamaria, making telling pacifist propaganda with the grave innocence of his children, their softly grained photo-lithographic images contrasted with the inkless embossing of bullet holes in doves, and daisies growing out of rifle barrels.

In late 1968, a hybrid image by Tetsuya Noda won the grand prize at the Tokyo Print Biennale, a posed family snapshot enlarged by photo-screen, with its members sitting inscrutably on a sofa exquisitely printed by traditional wood-block. The same

87

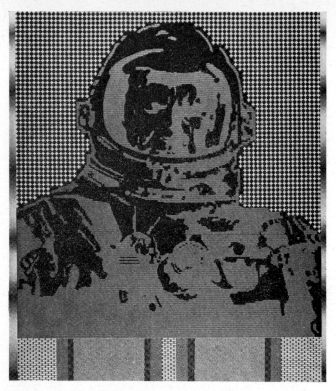

month, all three main prize-winners at the first British Print Biennale in Bradford had made creative use of photographic techniques : in fact six out of the total of ten prize-winners had, the student prize going to Michael Fossick, who reflected impressions of a technological world simply and cleverly in *Komtek I*, with assembled mechanical tints photographed on to a screen.

The Pole Roman Opalka, took the Arts Council prize with *Adam and Eve*, first in a brilliant cycle with sociological implications called *The Description of the World*. In *Adam and Eve* (who started the trouble, not to mention the population explosion), the photograph of a crowd detail is systematically reduced and the repetitions collaged, transferred to a sensitized etching plate, etched, then hand-finished. Companion image *The Tower of Babel* is a structure built from a world-wide variety of architectural styles, while in *The Deluge,* central skyscrapers, shrinking as they repeat outwards, amount to an effect like soil erosion after flood.

Michael Fossick *Komtek 1* 1968
Screenprint, edition 15, prizewinner Bradford Biennale, 1968

Roman Opalka *Adam and Eve* 1968
Etching, edition 10, prizewinner Bradford Biennale, 1968

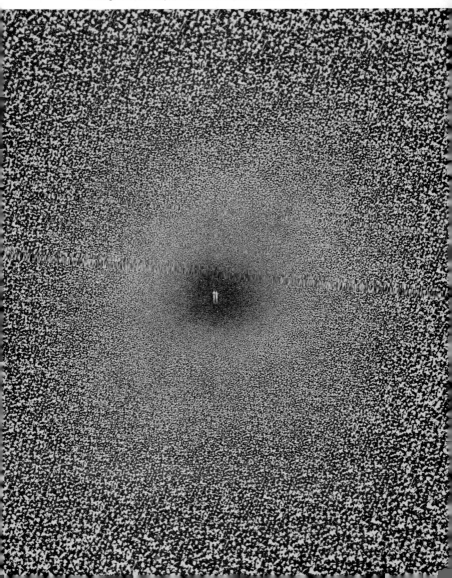

Colin Self *Out of Focus Objects and Flowers 3* 1968
Etching, edition 75, prizewinner Bradford Biennale, courtesy Editions Alecto,
London

Colin Self, another of Bradford's main winners, entered an
oval silver vignette, nostalgic for the 1940s, in which the burnished
etched ghosts of flowers, and soft-ground tinsel, were surmoun-
ted by a mackerel sky obtained by inverting a wave photograph.
One can perhaps explain the choice of this piece for the Biennale
by its preponderance of hand-work, rather than the synchronous
Power and Beauty series in which Self's debt to photography is
more obvious, re-presenting images he had compulsively collected, and interfering artistically only in order to underline the
mechanical force of the originals. In fact, his artistic adjustments
in size, colouring, and technique, have done this in remarkable
ways: the sinister elephantine quality of an American customized
car is etched with slaggy half-tone dots on silver; the trichromatic
separations of the screenprinted peacock include a white printed
first through the cyan screen, frosting the feathering and empha-
sizing the intense blue of the bird's plumage.

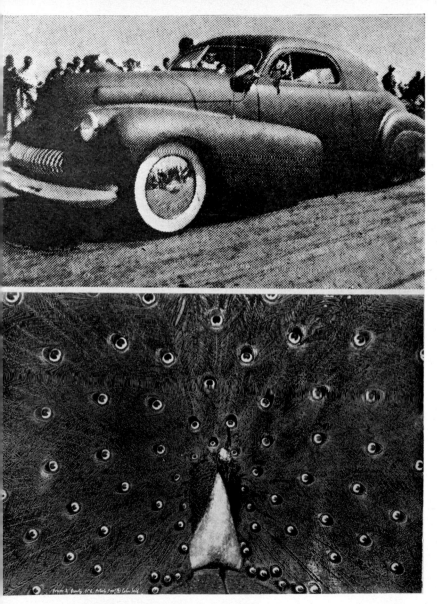

Colin Self *Power and Beauty* series, 1968
(Above) *Car* Etching, edition 75
(Below) *Peacock* Screenprint, edition 75
Courtesy Editions Alecto, London

Mixed conventions

For some artists, as for American Warrington Colescott, 'drawing must always dominate', although his intaglio prints, contemplating the violence of society, past and present, are a complex of superimposed impressions which often include half-tone blocks. *Verdun-Defense* plays off cut-out hand-etched soldiers linked by blood-red barbed wire and ignited by silkscreened fluorescent flashes, against commercial letter-press plates, one showing a flock of sheep.

The tension arising when the studio product and the industrial confront each other, was noted by Michael Rothenstein in 1966 in *Frontiers of Printmaking*, and has been worked out powerfully in a number of combine-images such as *Through* where a photo-litho drill threatens the woundable surface of plank wood, rendered especially vulnerable by sensitive printing. Admitting that use of any photographic aid completely broke the recognized tradition in 'original' printing, he argued that an artist might nevertheless legitimately introduce one such element, among

Warrington Colescott *Verdun-Defense* 1968
Etching, aquatint and screenprint, edition 25, courtesy London Arts

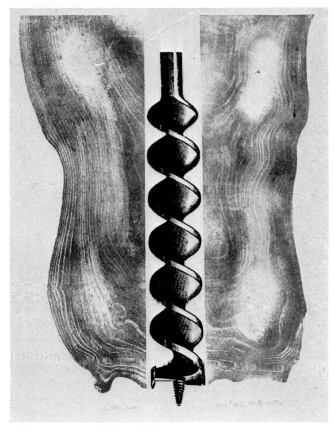

Michael Rothenstein *Through* 1968
Wood and photo-litho, edition 25, courtesy Bradford Biennale

others. He also remarked that the outdated 'originality' definitions
needed revising to include, in their own novel category, exclusively
photo-screenprints such as the remarkable *As is When* series Prater
had just completed for Paolozzi. But as a studio-based artist,
Rothenstein couldn't resist a final plea that all other things
being equal, an artist-printed print embodied 'a more total
originality'. Legend has it that *Formica-Formikel*, an image from
Paolozzi's following photo-screen undertaking, *Moonstrips*, was
dedicated to him to commemorate his tussle with a knotty
problem.

Carol Summers *Fontelimon* 1967
Woodcut, edition 60, courtesy Bradford Biennale
94

Chagall, *Daphnis and Chloe: La Leçon de Philétas* 1960
Lithograph, edition 60, Bibliothèque Nationale, Paris

95

Allen Jones *Life Class no. 2* 1968
Litho and photo-litho, edition 75, courtesy Editions Alecto, London

Allen Jones / James Wedge *Thrill Me* 1969
Litho and photo-litho, courtesy Editions Alecto, London

Hand-made and mechanical print combinations, whether to meet 'originality' halfway, or out of a wish to mix the conventions of industrial process and hand-work, have proliferated.

Allen Jones's *Life Class* directed a fashion model and professional photographer to avoid a collage situation, and provide the lower half of a series of seven split lithographs. The photographs of Moira Swan's legs in pearlized stockings were used full strength on the bottom half, and printed by photo-lithography, while Jones's autographic additions completed the upper half of the print and sometimes spilled over the photo-lithography too.

Jones's continuing admiration for the strength and involvement of the fetish magazine artist beside the weakness of art school life drawing, led to the print *Thrill Me*, a collaboration with photographer James Wedge, in which the problem once

Richard Hamilton
(Above) *I'm Dreaming of a White Christmas* 1967
Screenprint, edition 75, courtesy Petersburg Press, London
(Below) *My Marilyn* 1965
Screenprint, edition 75, courtesy Editions Alecto, London

more was to equal the photograph's power. A print of his hand-drawn stone lithograph beside Wedge's photograph of a nude dancer (her impact somewhat diminished by a trendy fig-leaf from dress designers Tuffin and Foale) was rephotographed and editioned, after colour separations, by photo-lithography.

Richard Hamilton, sometimes called the first Pop artist, whose obsession is 'to see conventions mix', wrote in the catalogue of the *This is Tomorrow* exhibition in 1956 : 'What is needed is not a definition of meaningful imagery, but the development of our perceptive potentialities to accept and utilise the continual enrichment of visual material.'

His analysis of mass media iconography and symbolism, and its integration with fine art, has displayed an esoteric grasp of methods and techniques in both, together with a taste for philosophical speculations about reality and illusion.

Several works were spawned by a Vista-Vision film *I'm Dreaming of a White Christmas*, from which a colour reversal negative film clip became a marvellously sensuous oil painting, with a preparatory work in watercolour. The latter was used for a screenprint selectively breaking down each wash of colour into as many as three separations without the use of half-tone, while the oil painting gave rise to a lithograph. Wreaking delicious havoc with the twentieth-century tenet 'truth to materials', the lithograph renders the oil almost photographic, while the screenprint derived from the watercolour is usually mistaken for a lithograph ; thus the image from the original clip has been batted creatively backwards and forwards between the conventions of lens formulation and eye interpretation, hand and eye continually adjusting the mechanical. Hand-mark and photograph are again compared in the photo-screen *My Marilyn*, a collage from photographs the star had approved or vetoed with ticks and crosses. The quality which makes Hamilton such a potent artist is the humanity surfacing other complex stratifications of meaning : Bing transformed by his looking-glass world to a black-shirted white-hatted American Negro is heady magic ; while the tragedy of a suicidal love-goddess, symbolized by her image attacked with crosses

meaning both cancellation and kiss, can bring a lump to the throat.

While most holiday photos bore, insignificant detail from Hamilton's can be made memorable. A tiny scrap of transparency snapped on a Greek island was blown up in steps, and screen-printed to Hamilton's specifications by Domberger of Stuttgart with an unusual trichromatic processing in which colour reversals and white introduced through a textural mesh added up to one of his most beautiful images; while, challenging the cliché of photographic truth, a portion of a postcard showing holiday-makers on the beach at Whitley Bay, was enlarged to the point where *People* became 'unreadable abstract clumps of silver halides'. Editioned as a photograph, the people are joined by sprayed and hand-painted marks, collage, Letraset, and black and white areas of screenprinting.

Hamilton's editioned photograph in a fine art context is comparatively rare. Although photographs have been editioned by other artists—Barry Flanagan, Sir George Pollock, for example —it is more common to pass photographic elements through other printing processes. The possibilities for photography in the fine art area, however, will undoubtedly be encouraged by

Richard Hamilton
(Above) *German Family in Greece* 1967
Screenprint, edition 75
(Below) *People* 1968
Photograph with screenprinting, collage, etc., edition 26
Courtesy Petersburg Press, London

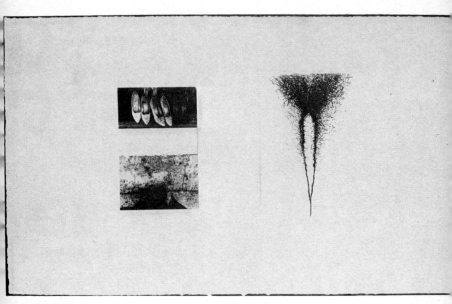

Jim Dine / Lee Friedlander *Exchanging Things* 1969
Photo by L.F., etching by J.D., edition 75, courtesy Petersburg Press, London

Exchanging Things, sixteen photographs by Lee Friedlander editioned with accompanying etchings, conveying a very personal vision, by Jim Dine. Perfectly matched, their images set up aesthetic and symbolic counterpoints: two tiny pairs of scissors beside a fragilely wire-fenced flower-bed; what might or might not be a hirsute carrot by Dine against Friedlander's forlorn array of empty shoes.

If in no other area, art has proved one in which the end will often more than justify the means.

THE DEMOCRATIC ART

Prints have often been called The Democratic Art. Carl Zigrosser, eminent American print historian, quotes the unknown author of a 1747 treatise on engraving as saying:

It requires a large Fortune to make a fine Collection of Paintings, and great Judgement to avoid Imposition, and understand their beauties, but Prints are adapted to all Ages, all Ranks of Men and all Fortunes; they cost much less than paintings, the knowledge of them is more easily attained, and they comprehend all Sorts of Subjects, they are equally as useful as entertaining. . . .

It was their usefulness or entertainment value (as religious images and playing cards) that made even the fifteenth-century man-in-the-street, short as he was of superfluous cash, a print purchaser. To-day, there are few citizens in Western society who, if they saved a little, could not afford to own a significant artist's editioned image for the sheer aesthetic joy of it. As Van Gogh wrote to Theo—print is a means of offering good art at low prices to the poor and middle classes.

It might be argued ironically that the 'equality' on which the proposition of a democratic art is based, actually means that a poor man can buy an inexpensive quantity production, while a privileged one can afford a unique work (so that some are more equal than others). The idea, however, that prints are the poor relations of painting and sculpture has succumbed gradually, as masterpieces otherwise inaccessible have originated in the various duplicating media and have, moreover, demonstrated that the only values which may be diminished by multiplicity are Stock Exchange values, not aesthetic ones.

Democratic principles have led to a wider sharing out of wealth and a broader basis for education, slowly producing a general public rich enough to afford and intelligent enough to appreciate art. Moreover, one supposes the artist of the future will depend on public support and understanding increasing, since with the decline of privileged patronage, large commissions may well spring primarily from State institutions or public corporations, whose funds, however tenuously, are democratically controlled; while in the private sector, the growing needs of the individual may be conveniently met by editioned art.

Before the last war, Hayter recalls that it was practically impossible to give modern prints away in America. Since 1945, increased awareness of communications has seen the flowering of world-wide dealer, biennale, atelier, and educational foundation systems devoted to their production and dissemination, and the print's mobility, needing only a cardboard cylinder to travel from one end of the world to another, has given artists (whose job after all is the communication of ideas by visual means) an ideal way of reaching far more people.

Internationalism

When the United States Information Agency toured a show, including abstraction, called *Graphic Arts USA* in Russia in the early 1960s, it scandalized the Russian press, and Madame Furtseva, then Minister of Culture, told the accompanying Americans: 'Art that cannot be understood by the people, is not art.'

Although in the West we deem most creative the artist who forces us to change our concepts, or see things in a new way (rather than comfortingly repeating what we already know), in nations still struggling materially, art is expected to reiterate useful social messages in the pragmatic situation.

A vital tradition, in a figurative art understood by the people, was established in Mexico by Posada, who died in 1913, having lived through the Mexican Revolution. Reputed to have made 20,000 prints, often from type-metal, he directly engraved some, and drew on others with a resist before relief etching them in a bucket of nitric acid.

Members of the Mexican Popular Graphic Art Workshop have followed his socially conscious figurative tradition, circulating many explicitly educational prints. Angelo Bracho, a founder

José Guadelupe Posada *Political Discourse*
Relief engraving, courtesy Brooklyn Museum, NY

Angelo Bracho *Rubber Collecting* 1958
Lino-cut, courtesy Ljubljana Biennale

member from 1937, who showed the vigorous lino-cut *Collecting Rubber* at the 1959 Ljubljana Biennale is typical of the school. Swamped by the rising tide of non-representational art, the Mexicans seem to have retired from international competition.

Vladimir Kutkin *My Country: Party right* 1967
Lino engraving, courtesy Ljubljana Biennale

The Russians, however, proscribed by officialdom, continue to
enter stylizations like Vladimir **Kutkin's** lino-engraved *Triptych—
My Country: Party left, Party right, and centre*—in which the
harmony and honest toil begin, artistically, to wear a little thin.

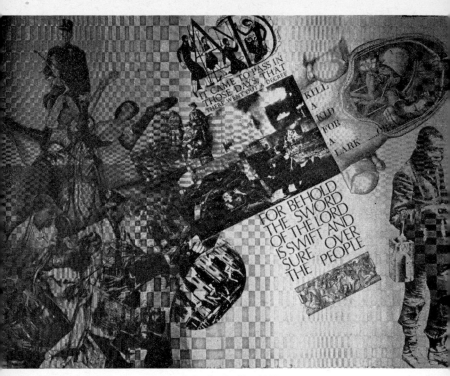

Bill Weege *Would'st thou have Daley for thy King* 1968
Screenprint and offset litho, edition 20, courtesy Bradford Biennale

A different kind of propaganda, individual criticism, lies in the protest art of American Bill Weege, whose photo-mechanical printing research has taught him how to strike fast. *Would'st thou have Daley for thy King*, a photo-screen and lithograph, linking sex with violence, news with entertainment, in condemnation of American society, was completed by Sunday afternoon after a Friday evening newscast that the Chicago Mayor had instructed his police to shoot during race riots. That Bradford Biennale awarded the print a prize supports the argument that in the West, whatever else is lousy about our system, we enjoy individual expressive freedom, for one can scarcely imagine a parallel situation, with the Cracow Biennale awarding a Russian a prize for a print questioning the authority of his State. Having slated Johnson with anti-Vietnam portfolios, Weege promised a series on the Nixon administration, if and when it ever made any policy decisions.

Weege's self-imposed task is more often fulfilled these days by the press cartoonist; indeed, Daumier's lithography succumbed to the Gillotype (a line block) over a century ago. But although he produces prints in a limited edition fine art context, Weege has often signed over their reproduction rights to unlimited poster firms; thus his polemics travel.

It's among the amusements of art history either to find evidence for international styles, or to struggle to see national coherence as one can in the continuing traditions of printed folk-art. Possibly one might pigeon-hole an unknown Russian's prints without hesitation, but such is the international interchange, both of prints and of artists, that few products of the myriad sub-cultures within our global village succumb any longer to simple analyses.

Sometimes, one feels, there is a special kind of Central European (Austrian, Czech, German) morbidity, manifested by the externalization of Surrealist fantasy, bred by childhood witness of death and destruction growing old in an age of spare-part surgery. Horst Janssen, who won the Venice Biennale Engraving Prize in 1968, makes membraneous etchings of contused or putrescent human beings, while, although Wunderlich can display a wry humour, his taste for depicting the crêpe of aged or decomposing skin with eddies of lithographic *lavis*, more often makes him look for something nasty in his woodshed.

Of all national schools, the modern woodcuts of the Japanese, combining calm, contemplative, two-dimensional abstraction with a genius for pattern, might, in the 1950s, have been said to have congruity, But even then, the passionate, almost *Fauve* expression and decoration of Munakata did not fit easily within the framework. In a class of his own, Munakata worked in a state of frenzy, almost attacking the wood-block with his tools, and he won many international prizes. Perhaps the love he shared with

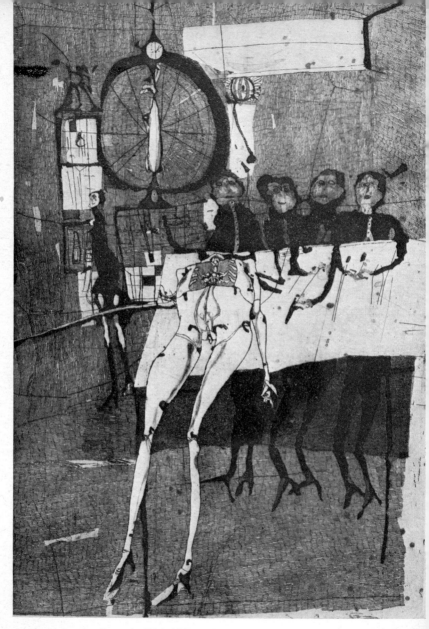

Horst Janssen *Anatomia di Tulp* 1958
Etching, courtesy Venice Biennale

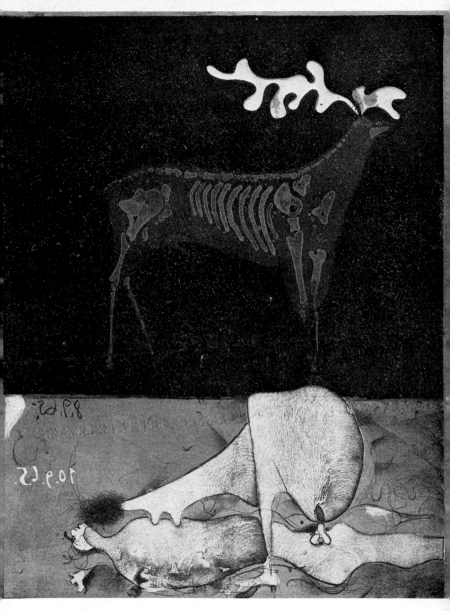

Paul Wunderlich *In the Dark Wood* 1965
Lithograph, courtesy Gallery Brusberg, Hanover

Munakata *Flower Hunting Mural* 1957
Woodcut, courtesy Robert Erskine

Kumi Sugai *Encres Bleues* 1963
Lithograph, edition 55, courtesy La Hune, Paris

his people for overcoming recalcitrant media helped to link him
with them. If so, then although Kumi Sugai's calligraphy pro-
claims Eastern origins, his choice of a painterly use of lithography
for the prize-winning prints of the early 1960s was again a
complete breakaway. Indeed, living in France, he was often
classified as *Ecole de Paris*. Latterly, Masuo Ikeda has collected

Masuo Ikeda *Half Marilyn* 1968
Lithograph, courtesy Fluorescent Chrysanthemum, ICA, London

Leon Piesowocki *Half-Moon Range* 1968
Woodcut, edition 70, courtesy Bradford Biennale

print prizes for Japan all over the world. Working on metal or stone, rare or non-existent media for his countrymen a generation ago, his imagery—the cover of *Life* magazine with Marilyn Monroe, women from *Vogue*, a cubed sky with a debt to Magritte —can confuse his exact origins. Yet *Half-Moon Range*, one would swear, exudes an air of Japan. Won only with effort from refractory materials—and incidentally printed by garden roller—it recalls Hokusai with the subtle starved edge inking, yet turns out to be the prize-winning woodcut of a Polish printmaker, Leon Piesowocki, who has lived twenty years in England.

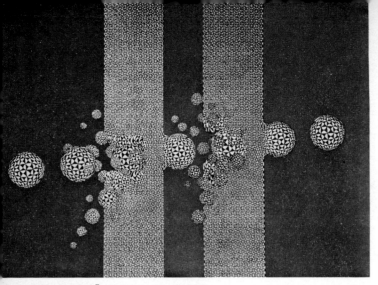

Miroslav Šutej *Composition III* 1967
Screenprint, courtesy Ljubljana Biennale

Modes of dissemination

Artists share printed ideas with the public by way of biennales,
publishing houses, and galleries, between themselves in group
ateliers of the kind made famous by Hayter.

The organized network now dealing exclusively with the dis-
semination of printed art has mushroomed unrecognizably since
World War II. Specialized open-print exhibitions started in
Switzerland—Bianco e Nero in 1950, Xylon Relief prints in 1953,
Grenchen Colour Print Triennial in 1955. But the first International
Print Biennale open to all comers and dedicated to the spirit of
international cooperation was in Ljubljana, Yugoslavia, in 1955,
the idea of Professor Zoran Kržišnik. Tokyo, Cracow, and now
Bradford have followed suit, with open international competi-
tions, while in Yugoslavia, the number of States and artists sub-
mitting prints has more than doubled over the years. The 1,000
prints of 1969, including impressive retrospectives by past prize-
winners Jasper Johns, Tapies, Hartung, and Dževad Hozo, not
only constituted a formidable achievement by their organization
and cataloguing but also suggested that by 1971, the spacious
Modern Gallery may no longer contain the entry. Ljubljana is the
printmaking centre of Yugoslavia, where graphic work is of very
116

Riko Debenjak *Traces no. 1* 1967
Etching and aquatint, courtesy Ljubljana Biennale

high quality. Although screenprinting has flowered there comparatively late, Šutej, for some time distinguished for his optically explosive geometrics, has recently added movable two-dimensional extensions to his prints, making them some of the most interesting to be seen, while Riko Debenjak, a leading international prize-winner, was accorded a major retrospective of his intaglio work in 1969 in which *Traces No. 1* marked a transition between a series exploring natural surfaces such as tree bark, conveyed by incisions and erosions in the plate, to more formal frameworks of subtle aquatinting, spectrally lit to suggest cosmic mirrors reflecting the magical dimensions of space.

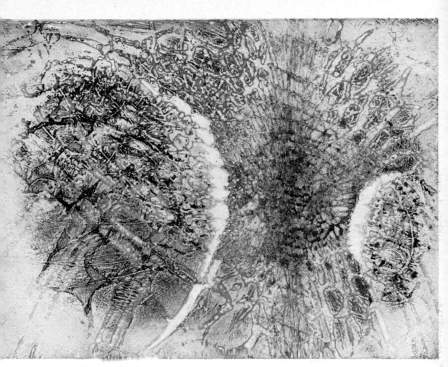

Krishna Reddy *Seed Pushing* 1968
Colour etching, artist's proof, courtesy Curwen Gallery, London

Johnny Friedlaender *Composition, variation in red* 1966
Etching and aquatint, edition 100, courtesy London Arts

In 1957 Debenjak worked in one of the Parisian intaglio ateliers run by the German Johnny Friedlaender. Distinguished artists and students on scholarships pass through such workshops, pooling ideas, and contributing to the international cross-fertilization. Friedlaender has been a very influential teacher, continuing to print colour by means of several registered aquatint plates, but making new use of contrived accidents in surface erosion. Krishna Reddy, of India, who worked at Atelier 17 as Hayter's *massier*, has made an individual addition to Hayter's one-plate technique, contriving opalescent colour effects of great beauty and complexity, altering the path of various rollers to travel either horizontally or vertically over the corrugations which characterize his work.

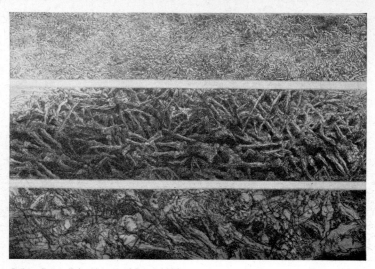

Gabor Peterdi *Landscape of Death* 1966
Etching and engraving, edition 25

Students from Hayter's American workshop fanned out all over the United States after World War II; Lasansky, for example, setting up an important print centre at Iowa University, and Gabor Peterdi, a Hungarian originally with Hayter in Paris, establishing a Graphic Workshop at the Brooklyn Museum in 1949. In his own work, sometimes haunted by grim experiences as a soldier in Europe, Peterdi more often affirms his faith in life by showing growth from decay.

Detailing all the American institutions to flower from Hayter's Atelier 17 seeds could make a book by itself. Some institutions, such as the Philadelphia Print Club, already existed, but blossomed yet more vigorously with comprehensive programmes of exhibitions, publishing, and workshops; the Brooklyn Society of Etchers burgeoned into the Society of American Graphic Artists. A Print Annual began at Brooklyn in 1947, the International Biennial of Colour Lithography (now defunct) at Cincinnati in 1950. In the late 1950s the Pratt Graphics Center in New York was set up, with the help of the Rockefeller Foundation, as a non-profit organization devoted to furthering ideas in all branches of creative printmaking. The Center typifies the best to be found in these communal workshops and its atmosphere was described

120

Romas Viesulas, score from *Metamorphoses* by Vladimir Ussachevsky and *Core* both from *Notes on Image and Sound* 1964/5
Inkless intaglios, edition 20 each

by a *New York Times* writer as a cross between a beehive, a picnic, and a religious observance performed with presses and acids instead of altars and libations.

Romas Viesulas, born in Lithuania, provides a one-man comprehensive survey of the foundations and grants America can bestow on her artists. A 1958 Guggenheim Fellowship permitted lithographic study with Desjobert in Paris. In 1960 he became the first artist to involve a Tamarind Fellowship and produced a portfolio called *Toro Desconocido* dedicated to all who give their lives in obscurity; a Tiffany Fellowship in 1962 resulted in *Hew* based on Mayan and Aztec mythology learnt from travels in Mexico; while another Guggenheim Fellowship at the American Academy in Rome in 1964/65, gave birth to a group of inkless reliefs and lithographs called *Notes on Image and Sound*. This portfolio was inspired by contemporary experimental music with five of the images from composer's scores using new visual symbols simply transcribed into inkless relief and five related interpretations of their sound, by Viesulas. Fourteen different institutions the length and breadth of America purchased part or complete sets of this undertaking, such is the network of print collections.

The Tamarind Fellowship, backed by the Ford Foundation, was the idea of June Wayne, who wanted to bring back the stone age by resuscitating the dying craft of the hand-pulled lithograph. Artists, fully fledged but needing technical assistance, are invited to spend two months at the Hollywood workshop, making editions of twenty-nine prints, with twenty for themselves, nine for Tamarind. The *bon à tirer* (the artist's 'OK-to-go' proof) belongs to the printer, for the Fellowship provides advanced schooling for him as well.

Normally an artist spends one month with master-printer Clifford Smith, the second with apprentices. *The Fourteen Stations of the Cross* made there by sculptor Robert Cremean to explore the concept of group dogma destroying the individual, was so demanding, however, that the whole of his time had to be spent with the master-printer. After specially pulling five hundred 'flats' to give Cremean the unusual butcher-paper brown background he wanted, continuity and precision were the watchwords, for a sensitive line, like an engineering drawing with its isometric projections, definitions of axes, and diagrammatic symbols of force and thrust, had to be registered with areas of gradually deepening pink, suffusing to maximum intensity at Christ's third fall, thereafter waning.

Tamarind, scheduled to be dismantled in Spring 1970, will be parent to lithography workshops all over America. Already several ex-Tamarind printers—De Soto, Irwin Hollander—have begun workshops of their own, and a former Technical Director, Ken Tyler, has established Gemini at Los Angeles. In addition to publishing the work of distinguished artists he undertakes research and experiment which absorbs a quarter of Gemini's time. He expressed the opinion that only crafts which learn to adopt technology and develop new hybrids will succeed, while craftsmen steeped in archaic traditions and with one or both feet in the past, will die. His technical competence and innovation have been amply demonstrated in Stella's *Star of Persia* prints, critically registered on graph paper and using newly developed metallic flake pigmentation in the inks, and Albers's *White Line Squares*,

Robert Cremean *Stations of the Cross 3 and 11* 1967
Lithographs, edition 29 each

an exhausting eleven-month project, demanding not only accurate flat colours of great purity but crisp hairlines within colour areas, with the surrounding inks printed without perceptible overlap.

Jasper Johns *Black Numeral 3* 1968
Lithograph, edition 70, courtesy Gemini GEL, California

Two other leading American artists, Rauschenberg and Jasper Johns, have made outstanding prints at Gemini: Rauschenberg with his first essay into colour (and fluorescent colour at that) based on *Bonnie and Clyde*, Johns with a development of his *0–9 numbers*, designed to cover the spectrum of lithographic possibility, each exquisite print involving a stone carrying the imagery in opaque black, and a metal plate for a grey transparent overlay. Both artists have also worked with Tatyana Grosman, a Russian lithographer now established on Long Island, who, according to Allen Jones, identifies with her artists and has never produced a bad print. *L'Oeil* said of the work Johns produced there, that lithography had not been so well served since Odilon Redon. Now Mourlot, of Paris, has a branch in New York; the stone age has certainly had a revival.

In England the proximity of Europe with its craft traditions, and the decline of print trade after the hiatus of the depression and world war, meant that the only presses were in art schools. Work from artists teaching printmaking thus formed the initial source of supply for Robert Erskine when he founded the St George's Gallery in the 1950s, inspired by such European publishers as the Guild de la Gravure.

Erskine's contribution lay not so much in what he published— although he put out some excellent prints—but in doing the spade-work in public relations for the idea of editioned originals rather than reproductions. He had a genuine and attractive desire to produce good art cheaply for the general public, writing in an article in *Arts Review*: '. . . and I mean the Mums and Dads in Pinner and Wigan'.

As well as improving print presentation, banishing fingerprints from margins, he made a film on techniques, put British graphics on the map by touring exhibitions abroad, and imported shows from artists such as Hayter, Sugai, Munakata, and Baskin. His *Graven Image* shows from 1959 to 1962 eventually gained the support of Trust House Hotels, who sponsored five £200 prizes and patronized winning prints, although the real inroads he had made into public ignorance and apathy were demonstrated

Henry Moore *Seventeen Reclining Figures* 1963
Lithograph, edition 75, courtesy Curwen Gallery, London

Tadek Beutlich *Two Suns* 1962
Wood and lino-cut, courtesy Grabowski Gallery, London

in 1962 when two editions of prints which hadn't won prizes (one a wood and lino print by Tadek Beutlich closely related to *Two Suns*) were completely sold out.

Erskine's lasting gift to English printmaking, when he phased himself out of publishing and went back to his first love, archaeology, was Stanley Jones, a Slade student who, after a spell in Paris at Erskine's instigation, set up an artist's lithographic studio within the already commercially established Curwen Press. Ceri Richards's 1959 *Hammerklavier Suite*, its first production, put Britain among the top prize-winners at that year's Ljubljana Biennale. A steady programme of publishing including works by such distinguished artists as Henry Moore, has continued to emerge from the Curwen Studio, and their Gallery, opened in 1965, displays not only their own publications but prints from all over the world. In London now, most galleries have print departments, and perhaps ten survive mainly by marketing graphics.

127

David Hockney *Bedlam* from *Rake's Progress* 1961/3
Etching, edition 50, courtesy Editions Alecto, London

Editions Alecto began with an undergraduate subscription scheme for a John Piper print commemorating the 400th anniversary of Westminster School. Expanding, and inheriting Erskine's mantle in 1962, Alecto's first spectacular success was a *faux-naïf* up-dating of Hogarth's *Rake's Progress* by David Hockney, chronicling his adventures in America. Outlet galleries have now been established in London and New York, and a sophisticated publishing programme includes the production of editioned art objects. One of Alecto's founder-directors, Paul Cornwall Jones, has formed his own *avant-garde* publishing concern, the Petersburg Press.

Marlborough Fine Art also entered print publishing in the mid-sixties, impressed by the inclusion of British artists in European Graphic portfolios, such as those by Wolfgang Ketterer. Moore, Sutherland, Kokoschka, Tilson, Kitaj, and Piper have turned out a torrent of work for them, using Curwen and Kelpra Studios in London, and various Continental printers.

New style art dealing was started in Great Britain by American

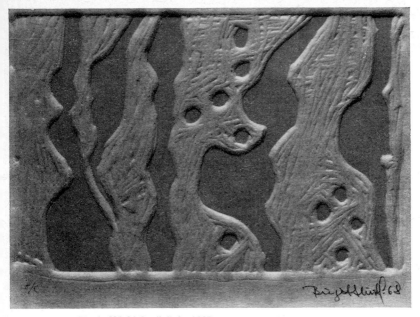

Birgit Skïold *Sunlit Ruins* 1967
Relief etching, edition 50, courtesy London Arts

Eugene Schuster. Financing the promotion of young artists by profits from old master prints, Schuster believes that art is a commodity to be marketed like any other consumer item, and that people outside the art centres should not a chance to see and buy. Consequently his travelling exhibitions have visited universities all over England and America, while the headquarters from which he began operations, a house in North London, has grown to fill galleries in Bond Street, Detroit, and New York. Using inexpensive prints to inculcate a taste for art-collecting in the young (and hoping sprats now will catch mackerels later) Schuster markets a number of College Editions from the regular artists whose work he commissions. One of these is Birgit Skïold, a Swedish printmaker running the only London print workshop to provide facilities for artists who do not have their own. Her print, *Sunlit Ruins*, combining a glowing yellow printed from its relief with deep etched uninked intaglio, represents, at £5, the kind of temptation Schuster likes to place in the way of the buyer whose taste is in advance of his income.

Art for the people

One of the attractive features in the art democratization process is that combustion is often fired because those in a position to do something about it want to share with others experiences they themselves find life-enhancing.

The motivation does not have to be unadulterated altruism: publishers who risk capital outlay for ideas with problematic hope of financial return; governments, or their agents, who sponsor artists without prescribing what they say; business patrons who do the same as a prestige move in public relations—all these can have, at root, a guiding benevolence.

In 1937, Contemporary Lithographs, directed by John Piper and Robert Wellington, published stone-drawn prints intended for schools, quoting a report on *Art in Education* which advocated an enriched stock of images in the child's environment to stimulate efforts at comparison and criticism. Graham Sutherland's *Sick Duck* was one of ten prints costing £8 the set, or 30s each framed. Gray called the venture 'one of the most hopeful events in the history of the English print'.

The war interrupted this project, but a similar one was pursued in 1949 by Mrs Brenda Rawnsley of School Prints Ltd. With the new lightweight plastic lithographic plates which had just come out, she conceived the idea of commissioning great living artists —Henry Moore at home, Braque, Matisse, Dufy, and Picasso in France—each to draw a six colour image, the resultant large editions of which would be offered inexpensively to educational authorities.

Indeed, to secure Picasso's collaboration, she even got airborne, chartering an aeroplane to Nice and keeping a mad *rendezvous* with him on the beach. Interested in the new materials, and intrigued by her aeroplane in which he nearly took a first flight, he recorded it in his composition, including Mrs Rawnsley in her sun-hat, eating a melon.

Education authorities were sluggish in snapping up the publications she offered them, large outstanding prints for which

Graham Sutherland *Sick Duck* 1936
Lithograph, edition 400, Contemporary Lithographs, courtesy Curwen Gallery, London

the artists signed a *bon à tirer*, but not individual sheets; however, in the longer term, enthusiasm for graphics has come to the boil, and Mrs Rawnsley's imaginative enterprise has not gone unrewarded.

Art for the people in Sweden has been highly organized since 1947, and Stenquist, who won a Xylon V prize with his *Mikrokosmos XIII*, is one of many artists whose graphic works are commissioned and circulated all over the country by the Society for Art Encouragement, especially in places outside the cultural mainstreams. Backed by the British equivalents of such organizations as the TUC, WEA, and educational bodies, and financed partly by government grant, partly by membership fees, and partly by sales, the organization has carried out huge cultural information programmes and has exhibited graphics and three-dimensional art objects in editions all over the country, notably at a *Multikonst* exhibition opening in a hundred centres simultaneously in 1967.

131

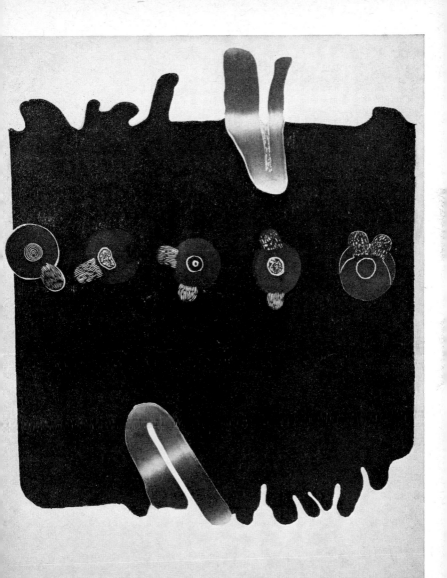

Stenquist *Mikrokosmos XIII* 1968
Lino engraving, courtesy Xylon, Switzerland

Henry Moore (above) *Sculptural Objects* ; **Picasso** (below) *Composition*
Lithographs by School Prints, edition 3000 each, 1949

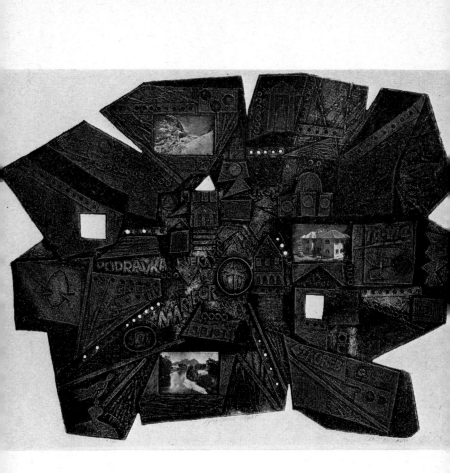

Clare Romano *Ljubljana Night* 1965
Collograph intaglio and relief, edition 60
134

Art, to be sent in the same way as material aid to underdeveloped areas, 'who presumably like and need pictures as much as we do', was the suggestion of Gustave von Groschwitz, curator of prints at Cincinnati in 1960, who thought the State Department should commission lithographs on zinc plates, and woodcuts to provide electrotypes, so that American printmakers could give something to the world. Certainly by using graphic art as diplomatic gifts, hanging it in Embassies, touring exhibitions of it and arranging cultural exchanges abroad, the State Department and the US Information Agency has done a great deal. Clare Romano's collograph *Ljubljana Night*, a collage of fabrics, papers, *objets trouvés*, and traditionally etched plates, stuck to cardboard with acrylics and inked both intaglio and relief, was made during 1965 while she was artist-in-residence on a cultural mission in Yugoslavia. Six days a week from 9 a.m. to 7 p.m. the team demonstrated, fraternized, and exuded good will, as a reporter put it : '. . . working in a public atelier before thousands of passers-by like the pancake turner in a diner'.

Similar schemes in the Soviet Union and Rumania, were obviously not motivated solely by a desire to provide art for the people. The Americans clearly hoped that by exporting friendly artists and exciting new print ideas, ordinary folk would think of them as goodies, rather than baddies. But as in Russia, where the press branded the US Graphics Exhibition 'an outrage', calculated risks may backfire.

In recent years large business corporations have been generous in distributing patronage, partly out of a feeling of responsibility and a desire to contribute to society, partly out of the knowledge that more people now visit museums than football stadiums and that good art will be identified with the good business that engendered it. The President of Philip Morris International, George Weissman, pointed out honestly in 1966 that such policies were 'hard-nosed profit-oriented' and invaluable for the publicity they elicited. A splendid set of thirty-two Pop screenprints—among them Warhol's newspaper cutting of *Jacqueline Kennedy*—appeared, thanks to the firm, in 1965, and, as multiple art, raised

Warhol *Jacqueline Kennedy I* 1965/6
Screenprint, edition 200, courtesy Pop Graphics, Personna International

controversy and critical discussion in eighteen concurrent exhibitions all over the world. Afterwards the sets of prints were
auctioned for charity, or given to collections such as the Arts
Council of Great Britain, when Charles Wilson of Personna
International, a British branch of the American company, said in
a corporate statement: 'As manufacturers of mass consumer
products, we are intrigued by art forms which cut across in-
tellectual and cultural barriers, appealing to people of every type
and from every place.'

136

Cutting across cultural barriers, bringing art experience casually to the everyday world, furthering the democratization of art by supporting artists interested in commercial production, and increasing the chances of art to activate the whole environment, were the expressed aims of the Welsh Arts Council programme in placing posters by leading artists on public sites throughout the principality.

Legs, by Allen Jones, in which a serious artist explores the vital techniques of commercial art, was one of their screenprinted poster commissions. Not all viewers were sure how to react, but discussion and thought were certainly provoked and art was provided to enrich the environment with no motive other than to contribute to the quality of existence.

Allen Jones *Legs* 1968
Screenprint poster, unlimited, courtesy Welsh Arts Council

The way the print has suddenly come into its own has many contributory factors, but one of the most powerful is its versatility. No longer a medium which exists by aesthetic charity on ideas from painting and drawing, it provides artists with images which can only be obtained through print, and it has qualities quite beyond the reach of other media.

As a matter of fact, other media now profit from *its* aesthetic philanthropy. While some painters employ print elements within paintings, others find the flat impersonal finish of screenprinting preferable to anything they could achieve manually. Yet the relief possibilities of intaglio and vacuum forming, the flexibility with which paper can be cut, torn, and folded, make for an over-lap with sculpture or the work no longer confined to the single plane.

Then, while the idealists can claim unlimited prints as a democratic mass-produced art for the people, investors know that not only have rare old master prints shown a better financial return than any other outlay but even in the short term, limited edition products of the 1960s from artists such as Hockney, Hamilton, and Moore have already trebled and quadrupled their publication prices.

In this context, the hand/machine controversy, assisted by print technology, has thrown up a number of interesting questions. Now that quantity and quality can co-exist without dilution of the artist's intention, can we at last concentrate on the real value of art, aesthetic rather than commercial?

Although The Print Council of America has pointed out that their 'original' print definition was intended 'more as a protection against deceptive fraud than as a touchstone for the selection and valuation of prints . . . and not at all to direct printmakers to make original prints, or any other kind of prints', the cumulative effect of this, and related definitions specifying hand-work, numbering and signing as criteria, has been inhibiting. Years ago, for example, Man Ray wanted publishing support to pioneer photographic print forms, and was dissuaded. Prejudice has retreated slowly, and in addition, intrinsically unlimited media confined within select limited editions have perpetuated the rarity/quality confusion. Not least of the factors involved in a fixed boundary for 'original' printing, is that Customs and Excise observe it in deciding between untaxed art and taxed reproductions. Great Britain's out-dated regulations decree prints must be hand-made or taxed as reproductions, and although enlightened interpreters of such regulations can do much to prevent stagnation, they cannot get round the fact that any edition exceeding seventy-five copies is taxable, whether it's hand-made or not. So if a dealer with democratic leanings tries to keep the price down with a large edition, the democratic government, alleged to support the arts, immediately forces the price up.

Wider criteria to discriminate between originals and reproductions should undoubtedly have been found, and nothing would have given better protection and education to the public than that each print, by law, had to bear, or be accompanied by, the name of its inventor, all relevant collaborators, full details of production method and publisher.

The print, nevertheless, seems to contain all contraries. The professional artist can range from a man who still lovingly hand burnishes his block, to one commanding technicians wielding highly complex equipment, worth thousands of pounds. Flat or three-dimensional, gestural or impersonal, the finished work can range from a lithograph in which every sneeze, thumbprint, or brushmark from the artist is faithfully recorded, as in a Miro, to *Random War*, made by programming a computer to draw repeated soldier images—the positions and sizes of which were controlled by a series of random numbers generated within the machine.

Many of Paolozzi's prints have looked ahead intuitively to the Cybernetic Revolution. His collaboration with Prater on *As is When* paralleled that of the computer graphic which separated the conceptualizer (Professor Csuri of Ohio State University) and technician (programmer James Shaffer). Paolozzi's colour permutations, resulting in unique combinations in each print, are also akin to the random decisions of the computer to place,

Computer graphic *Random War* 1967
Courtesy Motif Editions, London

Miro *Oiseau Fronde* 1967
Lithograph, edition 75, courtesy London Arts

kill, or wound the soldiers. With such a graphic, it is possible either to produce identical prints, or produce prints with endless variations. In industry, expensive jigs once gave standardized flow-line mass products, but there are now numerically controlled machines which can obey tape-fed individual instructions: variety is being built in. It is not too far-fetched to imagine a cybernetic art of the future in which the conceptual artist will have a machine programmed to allow each individual to dial his own art-work and possibly to make decisions determining its form within set limits, making the spectator an active participant. Paolozzi has already divined this, by suggesting an owner of *Moonstrips* might cut up his images and reshuffle them.

Par Gunnar Thelander *Fly* 1967
Etching, edition 40

Prints have interesting contributions to make in art's dialogue
between illusion and reality. A mere drawing could not quite
equal the *trompe l'oeil* of Gunnar Thelander's *Fly* which, exactly
life-size, is the sole occupant of a sheet of paper, its etched
relief as palpable as the insect itself. On the other hand, the
tendency for artists to combine real things in their works has a
simple parallel in print where an exact impression of an object is
often a tolerable substitution for it (ensuring, moreover, that in an
edition of a dozen prints Bernd Löbach would not run out of
combinations!). Although one cannot imagine either of these
prints appearing before the twentieth century the techniques are
not new. In the last: 'The garment is spread over with print-colour;
after that is the garment covered with paper. Squeezes from my
hands, and the print is ready.'

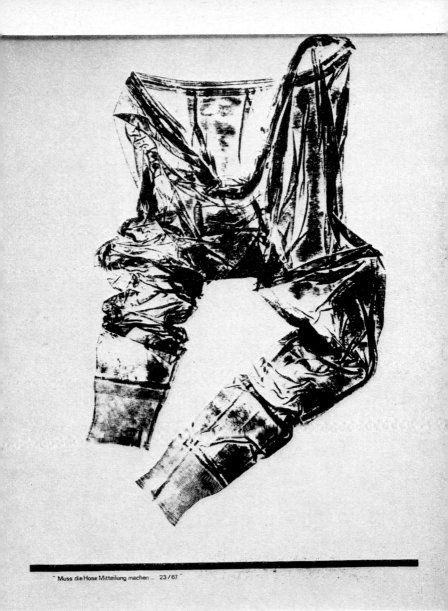

" Muss die Hose Mitteilung machen... 23/67 "

Bernd Löbach *Muss die Hose Mitteilung machen... 23/67* 1967
Material print, edition 12

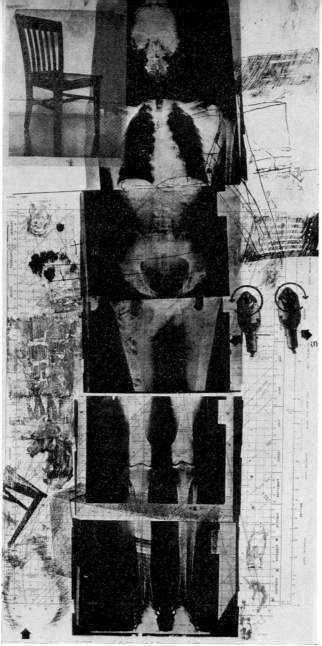

Left
Rauschenberg
Booster 1967
Lithograph and
silkscreen, edition 38,
courtesy Gemini GEL,
California

John Randolph Carter
Soldier 1968
Screenprint, edition 20

Rauschenberg's 6 × 3 feet maxiprint from the *Booster and Seven Studies* series is infinitely more complex in its components, while its attempt at universality arises from a philosophy that art, like life, is inexplicable. 'I do not know what it means, but its tone delights me,' is supposed to have been said of a foreign poem by Wittgenstein, and his remark could operate here. Among other things, the print includes a complete set of X-ray photographs of Rauschenberg, nude save for hob-nailed boots, zinc-cuts from a newspaper morgue, rubbings from newsprint echoing those in his *Dante* drawings, and technical manual illustrations silkscreened on to the stone. Once the entire assemblage had been lithographically printed, an astronomical chart for 1967, published by the University of Maryland, was superimposed, screenprinted in red enamel.

This unique ability of the print, to combine fragments of a different order into a single image, has attracted many artists. John Randolph Carter, for instance, says he wishes to establish

145

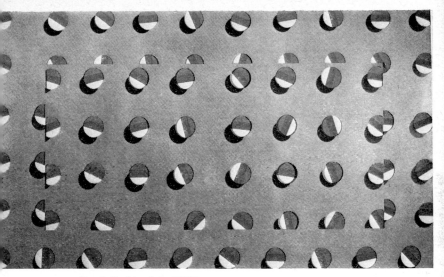

Derek Boshier *Output* 1966
Screenprint and collage, edition 75, courtesy Editions Alecto, London

Jim Dine *Tool Box no. 9* 1966/7
Screenprint and collage, edition 150, courtesy Editions Alecto, London

a brand-new identity for found images collaged together, and
that by printing them on a fresh sheet of paper, he can erase
their edges. Components from science fiction, children's books,
and food-cans, with photos from a book on Boston gardens, are
thus established in a perfectly flat new world.

The twentieth-century attitude to pictorial space permits the
use of different planes within an image. In his *Tool Box Suite*,
Dine, perhaps representing 'reality' with a photographic image
from a trade catalogue, screenprinted it, tore it, collaged it to
another sheet, then united the two with the black squiggle.
Derek Boshier, on the other hand, in *Output*, harnesses optical
flukes by screenprinting two sheets of paper and convinces you
that the central section, which is actually behind, appears in
advance of the foreground sheet.

David Hockney *Picture of a Landscape in an elaborate gold frame* 1965
Lithograph, edition 85, courtesy Editions Alecto, London

Those artists interested in the possibilities of translating marks
from one convention to another find print extends their area of
operations. Hockney, who says 60% of his work concerns technical devices, is fond of placing pictures within pictures, of trans-
posing a printed image, perhaps from an estate agent's brochure,

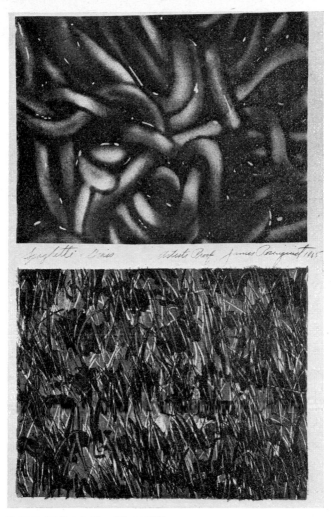

Rosenquist *Spaghetti and Grass* 1965
Lithograph, edition 23, courtesy Leo Castelli, New York

into deadpan paint, or a painted image into print. His ornately framed 'landscape' mocks a Hollywood fine art collection, using pictorial clichés translated into lithography. Rosenquist uses the tricks of advertising art to give impact to his representations of *Spaghetti and Grass*, while Lichtenstein sends up the splash and

Lichtenstein *Brushstrokes* 1967
Screenprint, edition 300, courtesy Leo Castelli, New York

Ronald King *Lulu* 1968
Screenprint on linen, edition 75, courtesy Canonbury Banner Company,
London

trickle of Abstract Expressionist paint, by the very deliberate screenprinted image, carefully imitating a cartoon drawing coarsely reproduced in half-tone letterpress printing. Thus while one is made aware of fresh discrepancies between reality and its representation, various conventions, formerly thought the vulgar and brazen province of commercial art, reveal their appeal assimilated into the fine artist's repertoire.

So barriers between disciplines go down, and prints prove adaptable in such amalgamations. In the poetry/poster *Offering Flowers*, Ian Tyson's complex histogram and typographic setting captures the mood and makes visual analogy with an Aztec poem, translated by Jerome Rothenberg. Ron King's richly sonorous *Lulu*, was one in a series of banners screenprinted on to dowelled linen and protectively coated, enabling it to be hung without glazing or framing, an ingenious half-breed, part Oriental scroll, part painting.

150

THE AZTECS HAD A FEAST WHICH FELL OUT IN THE 9TH MONTH AND WHICH THEY CALLED: THE FLOWERS ARE OFFERED.

& two days before the feast, when flowers were sought, all scattered over the mountains, that every flower might be found

& when these were gathered, when they had come to the flowers and arrived where they were, at dawn they strung them together; everyone strung them

& when the flowers had been threaded, then these were twisted and wound in garlands ......
long ones, very long, and thick ... very thick

& when morning broke the temple guardians then ministered to UITZILOPOCHTLI; they adorned him with garlands of flowers; they placed flowers upon his head

& before him they spread, strewed and hung rows of all the various flowers, the most beautiful flowers, the threaded flowers

then flowers were offered to all the rest of the gods

they were adorned with flowers; they were girt with garlands of flowers

flowers were placed upon their heads, there in the temples

& when midday came, they all sang and danced

quietly, calmly, evenly they danced

> they
> kept
> going
> as
> they
> danced

I offer flowers. I sow flower seeds. I plant flowers. I assemble flowers. I pick flowers. I pick different flowers. I remove flowers. I seek flowers. I offer flowers. I arrange flowers. I thread a flower. I string flowers. I make flowers. I form them to be extending, uneven, rounded, round bouquets of flowers.

I make a flower necklace, a flower garland, a paper of flowers, a bouquet, a flower shield, hand flowers. I thread them. I string them. I provide them with grass. I provide them with leaves. I make a pendant of them. I smell something. I smell them. I cause one to smell something I cause him to smell. I offer flowers to one. I offer him flowers. I provide him with flowers. I provide one with flowers. I provide one with a flower necklace. I provide him with a flower necklace. I place a garland on one. I provide him a garland. I clothe one in flowers. I clothe him in flowers. I destroy one with flowers. I destroy him with flowers. I injure one with flowers. I injure him with flowers.

I DESTROY ONE WITH FLOWERS; I DESTROY HIM WITH FLOWERS; I INJURE ONE WITH FLOWERS: with drink, with food, with flowers, with tobacco, with capes, with gold.

I beguile, I incite him with flowers, with words; I beguile him, I say, 'I caress him with flowers. I seduce one. I extend one a lengthy discourse. I induce him with words.'

I provide one with flowers. I make flowers, or I give them to one that someone will observe a feastday. Or I merely continue to give one flowers; I continue to place them in one's hand, I continue to offer them to one's hands. Or I provide one with a necklace, or I provide one with a garland of flowers.

From original NAHUATL texts recorded by BERNARDINO DE SAHAGÚN C16th, in the FLORENTINE CODEX; arranged by JEROME ROTHENBERG from translations by ARTHUR J O ANDERSON & CHARLES E DIBBLE, & printed in J Rs TECHNICIANS OF THE SACRED, DOUBLEDAY & CO NY. ALL RIGHTS RESERVED

Ian Tyson *Offering Flowers* 1967
Screenprinted poetry/poster, edition 100, courtesy Circle Press, London

Kusaka *Work 68.9* 1968
Woodcut, courtesy Xylon, Switzerland

Robyn Denny *Suite 66, II* 1966
Screenprint, edition 75, courtesy Editions Alecto, London

Such is the impact of the machine age, that even employing traditional wood-block, the Japanese Kusaka seems to translate the rhythm of the sea into bold abstraction with only marginally more surface tactility than the screenprints by Robyn Denny. In the hand versus machine debate, screenprinting has incontrovertibly proved that absence of personal handwriting in no way diminishes the presence of the artist in the work. Prints by Paolozzi, Albers, Anuskiewicz, or Vasarely are easily identified. Similarly, Denny's work, with its symmetrical mazes and close chromatic

harmonies, is unmistakable. Such is his desire to remove all trace of the hand, that he has had identical images in different colour combinations screenprinted on to canvas as small paintings. Pol Bury too, using a photographic image of *Washington Bridge* and strategically cutting concentric circles to create an unstable *cinetization*, had it screenprinted on canvas in an edition of twelve. The border between printing and painting gets increasingly difficult to discern.

Pol Bury *Washington Bridge, Cinetization* 1966
Screenprint on canvas, edition 12, courtesy Kasmin Gallery, London

Richard Smith *Edward Gordon Craig no. 1* 1968
Lithograph, cut and folded, edition 95, courtesy Petersburg Press, London

Opposite
Yago Pericot *Cut and folded print* 1968
Etching and aquatint, courtesy Gerald Forty

Jasia Reichardt wrote in 1965 that one might soon walk into an exhibition of sculpture and find that all the exhibits were prints. Sure enough, the diversity of legitimate print materials and processes has allowed them to assume an extra dimension. Many prints have to be bought with a custom built frame; Allen Jones's *New Perspective on Floors*, for example, was designed to be folded into right-angled frames as a neat comment on Renaissance mathematics. Richard Smith has cut and folded his lithographs after printing to add actual dimension to an illusory theatrical depth, while Yago Pericot has etched, then cut and folded, a flat sheet to construct a three-dimensional chequerboard of nooks and crannies.

Joe Tilson *Two Wristwatches* 1965
Plastic vacuum forming, flocked and chromium plated, edition 35, courtesy
Marlborough Fine Art Ltd, London

Vacuum forming in plastic is now widely used to construct deep
reliefs with a technique little different, except in scale, from the
uninked gaufrage of Japanese embossing. Tilson's print *Two
Wristwatches*, flocked and chromium-plated, is an early example
160

Joe Tilson *Transparency: Che Guevara* 1968
Screenprint on acrylic and cellulose on wood relief, edition 20, courtesy
Marlborough Fine Art Ltd, London

of the use of the process, while his *Che Guevara*, materializing
in a combination of the idioms from which we know him—news-
reel and newspaper half-tone imitated by screenprint on acetate—
is framed in the deep relief of a simulated slide transparency.

Richard Smith first produced his *Sphinxes*, conceived frontally, as 'three-dimensional screenprints'. At last, however, in this free standing sculptural form we have something that, although it has print expansion to thank for its existence, is moving outside the scope of this book. Multiples is the term the art world has coined to such three-dimensional editioned art objects. Conceived for industrial techniques, idealists maintain their production should be unlimited.

There have been multiples for a long time: books could be called authors' multiples, gramophone records composers' multiples, and films playwrights' multiples, all, interestingly enough, dependent on print processes. Print is the great multiplier of art forms.

When it comes to multiples in the visual arts, however, no one can quite decide where a print ends and a multiple begins. But even when indisputably three-dimensional, it's curious how often the production of objects in editions involves elements of the printerly. Denny's *Colour Boxes* are layers of screenprinted acetate locked in a frame; Peter Sedgley's *Videorotors*, specially lit motor-driven discs, carry fluorescent screenprints which in movement fizz dizzily like phosphorescent flowers; one could go on. . . .

Richard Smith *Sphinx 4* 1967
Three-dimensional screenprint, edition 50, courtesy
Editions Alecto, London

Such objects are comparatively expensive however, and my favourite printed supermarket multiple is not. Diter Rot's slice of genuine banana sits cn a printed table (*reality and illusion; the unique and the mass-produced*). Although accompanying literature suggested fruit flies might invade the plastic box through a specially pierced hole, so far no English flies have been slim enough (*art/life continuum; the subversion of good taste*). However, the fruit has altered daily, expanding with an efflorescence of pink and grey-green mould, a velvet bloom I had not realized would be so fascinating (*through art, the ugly becomes beautiful*). One day, I imagine, the banana will dry out, and crumble to dust (*anti-museum, anti-investment*). This banana/ print has worried some, who refuse to equate art with rotting fruit on cheaply printed tables (*'Disgusted', Cheltenham*) but others it has intrigued, inviting philosophical speculations on the nature of art and the effects of change and time; which take us, of course, into the fourth dimension. . . .

Diter Rot *Table and Banana* 1969
Print in plastic box with banana, unlimited edition, courtesy
Vice-Versand, Wolfgang Feelisch, Remscheid, Germany

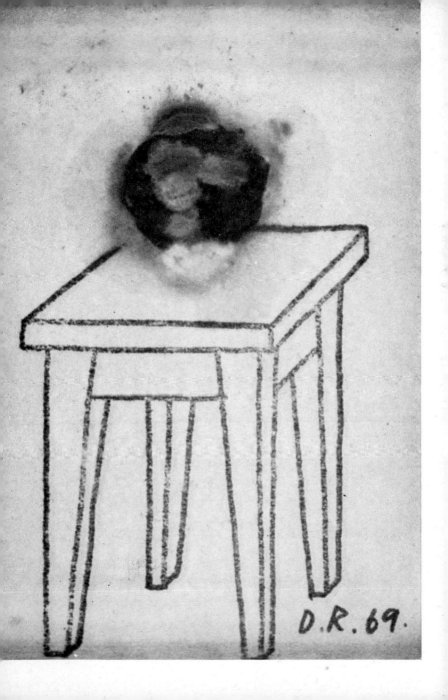

Book list

Artist's Proof (annual magazine) Pratt Graphics Center, New York

Bliss, D. P. *History of Wood Engraving* J. M. Dent, London, 1928

Cahn, J. B. *What is an Original Print* (pamphlet) Print Council of America, New York, 1961

Curwen, Harold *Processes of Graphic Reproduction in Printing* Faber & Faber, London, 1934

Gray, Basil *The English Print* A. & C. Black, London, 1937

Hayter, S. W. *About Prints* Oxford University Press, London, 1966

Hayter, S. W. *New Ways of Gravure* Oxford University Press, London, 1966

Ivins, William *Prints and Visual Communication* Harvard University Press, Cambridge, USA; and Routledge and Kegan Paul, London, 1953

Ivins, William *How Prints Look* Metropolitan Museum, New York, paperback 1943

Johnson, Una *Ten Years of American Prints 1947–56* Brooklyn Museum, New York, 1956

Jones, Stanley *Lithography for Artists* Oxford University Press, London, 1967

Man, Felix *150 Years of Artists' Lithographs 1803–1953* Heinemann, London, 1953

Peterdi, Gabor *Printmaking Methods Old and New* Macmillan, New York, 1959

Rothenstein, Michael *Linocuts and Woodcuts* Studio Vista, London, 1962

Rothenstein, Michael *Frontiers of Printmaking* Studio Vista, London, 1962

Scharf, Aaron *Art and Photography* Allen Lane, The Penguin Press, Harmondsworth, 1969

Sotriffer, K. *Printmaking, History and Technique* Thames & Hudson, London, 1968

Stubbe, Wolf *History of Modern Graphic Art* (to 1959) Thames & Hudson, London, 1963

Zigrosser, Carl *The Book of Fine Prints* Crown, New York, 1948

Zigrosser, Carl, with C. M. Gaehde *Guide to the Collecting and Care of Original Prints* Arco, London, 1965

Index

Italicized numbers refer to pages including illustrations

STUDIO VISTA/DUTTON PICTUREBACKS

edited by David Herbert